Spring Boot Primer

Second Edition

An introduction to Spring Boot so you won't regret it

If you have this book in your hands, you may have plans to develop with Spring(Spring Boot) in the future.

Everyone feels anxiety and fear when trying something for the first time. (At the same time, you may feel excited). But that's a good thing. Because we strive to drown out the anxiety.

Whatever the reason, trying new things leads to growth. The more unknown it is, the greater the degree of growth. Therefore, for you who have taken that step, growth is waiting for you.

When I started learning about Spring, I bought a number of Spring-related books (because I was afraid). But I didn't have a satisfying book. With the intention of changing that situation, we published the first edition of this book in 2018. Since Spring is also evolving, I have published the second edition.

In this book, you will use Spring to create one web application. Start by learning from the basics of Spring and gradually complete your application. By doing this, you will be able to acquire not only Spring but also the knowledge necessary for web development.

In other words, you can level up from knowing nothing about web development to being able to master Spring at once.

However, this book emphasizes practice rather than theory. There are various learning methods, but actually experiencing it is one of the efficient ways to learn. This is because it is scientifically known that the output has a high retention rate of knowledge. Also, when you actually make it and execute it, your anxiety and fear will disappear, so you will gain confidence.

It is better to actually move your hands to make it, but at first it is okay to just read a book. Since all the sample code can be downloaded, you can create an application even from the middle.

In the second edition

I am very pleased to receive highly rated reviews since the first edition of this book was published.

[Review of the 1st edition]

Spring Boot Primer: [Hands-On] Learn spring boot from the basics. An introduction to Spring Boot so you won't regret it Kindle Edition

by Tatsuya Tamura (Author)   Format: Kindle Edition

★★★★☆ ˅   8 ratings

> See all formats and editions

Kindle
$9.59

Read with Our **Free App**

   Kindle Customer

★★★★★ **Great, great, great book!!!**
Reviewed in the United States on January 12, 2021
Verified Purchase

This book is very easy for me to understand.
I recommend this book for all spring beginners.
All examples are very very helpful.
I want to buy the author's another books.
Tatsuya Tamura, you did a great job!!!

   Fernando P.

★★★★★ **Love this book**
Reviewed in Spain on March 28, 2021
Verified Purchase

A good introduction to Spring Boot.
Includes exception handling, Centralized logging, Rest services, internationalization, thymeleaf, JDBC and MyBatIs.

In the second edition I have the following modifications.

- Added contents about MyBatis and JPA
- Modified REST to be more practical
- Supports SpringBoot 2.4

These are the functions that are often used in the development field. Therefore, more practical content is increasing.

Thoroughly pursue clarity!

In this book, it has been described as follows in order to facilitate understanding.

- **Incorporate many illustrations**

  The ease of understanding changes greatly depending on whether or not there is a diagram at the time of explanation. For this reason, this book contains many illustrations to make it easier to understand.

- **Step by step**

  There are some things to keep in mind when teaching something. That is to tell only one thing. Being told multiple things at the same time can be confusing. Besides, books can only explain with letters and figures. Therefore, I will tell you one by one.

- **Clarify goals**

  Before actually making the sample code, I will explain what to make first. For example, ask them to create an application after explaining the contents with a screen image. Understanding is better if you know your goals.

We also put a lot of effort into explaining DI (Dependency Injection). Other books explain DI for advanced Java users and experienced Spring users. However, this book describes DI so that even Java beginners can understand it.

Structure of this book

Read this book in order, starting with Chapter 1, as you will gradually build your application. For example, first display the Hello World, then validation (input check), then screen layout, then database operation, and so on.

Target audience

In reading this book, it is desirable to have the following knowledge.

- Java basics
- HTML basics
- SQL basics

Basic level knowledge is sufficient.

Application configuration

The Web application developed in this document will be created with the following configuration.

- Spring: 5
- Spring Boot: 2.4.1
- Database: H2

* This is the latest version at the time of writing.

Now, try this book.

Table of Contents

1. Overview of Spring

This chapter describes an overview of Spring.

1.1 What is Spring?

Spring is a framework for Java development. Previously there were several frameworks. However, it is common sense to use Spring for the framework of Java development. This is because it is easier and faster to develop than other frameworks. It's also feature-rich, so it's ready for any project.

1.1.1 What is a framework?

Let's first consider the case where we don't use a framework. In this case, build the application from scratch. For example, suppose you create a login function. In this case, it is necessary to create a program that retrieves user information from the DB and verifies the password.

Now consider a framework. The framework provides some common features in advance. Developers create only those parts of the function that they want to change. The framework then calls the program for that change. For the login function, the developer only creates SQL to retrieve user information. The framework provides other processing.

[Figure] What is the framework?

【If you don't use a framework】

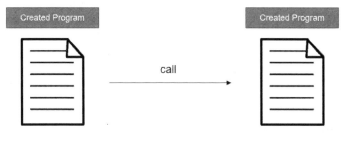

【When using a framework】

In other words, using the framework, you can create an application simply by creating the necessary part of the program. Since there is no need to create all the programs, the development efficiency will increase. So it is common sense to use frameworks in development.

Incidentally, the side from which the created program is called is called "Inversion of Control" (IoC for short). This idea can also be seen in DI (Dependency Injection)

1.2 What is Spring Boot?

Spring Boot is a framework that saves you the trouble of initializing Spring.

Before the introduction of Spring Boot, development sometimes stopped at the initial setting of Spring. This is because it is necessary to prepare an xml file in order to use the functions provided by Spring. Since it required specialized knowledge such as how to write an xml file, it took a long time to make the initial settings.

To solve the problem, Spring Boot was created. In Spring Boot, you simply select the functions you want to use in your application. After that, Spring Boot will automatically perform the initial setup. You can easily change the setting by simply changing the value of the property. Spring Boot is now used because it can improve development efficiency.

And compare this with cake making is as follows.

- **Spring**
  This is just the alignment of the cascading material.

- **Spring Boot**
  If you choose the ingredients for making the cake, the cake will be made to some extent. All you have to do is put strawberries and make various decorations.

2. Building the Development Environment

Before creating a program, let's build a development environment.

Spring has two types of eclipse. One is normal eclipse. Normal eclipse adds a plugin. The other is a Spring-specific eclipse. Both eclipse functions the same. Both methods of setting are listed, so please choose the one that is easy to use.

- Normal eclipse
- Install Spring-specific eclipse
- Install the Lombok
- Creating a Project

2.1 Normal eclipse

If you use normal eclipse, add a plugin. You can then develop with Spring. The latest eclipse may already have Spring plugins installed. First, make sure that the plug-in is installed. Do the following:

Choose Help > Eclipse Marketplace.

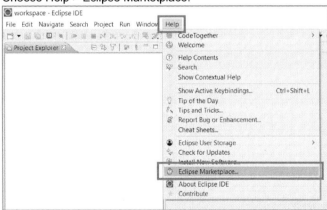

Type "spring" in the search field. If the Spring tool displays Installed, the Spring plug-in is installed.

If the plug-in has already been installed, configure the settings in [2.3 Install the Lombok]. If you have already installed Lombok, configure the settings in [2.4 Creating a project]. If the plug-in is not installed, make the following settings.

Select Install for the Spring tool.

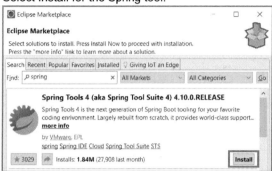

Check all and select "Confirm".

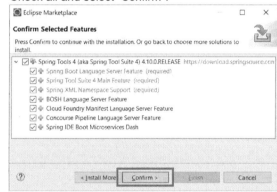

Accept the license and click Finish.

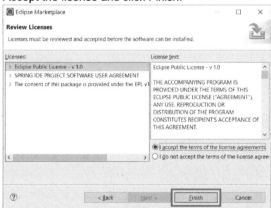

The plug-in will be installed after a while. Then restart eclipse. Next, configure the settings in [2.3 Install the Lombok]. If you have already installed Lombok, configure the settings in [2.4 Creating a project].

2.2 Install Spring-specific eclipse

The eclipse dedicated to Spring is called SpringToolSuite. Initially, it is called STS. This section describes how to install STS. Since the JDK is not included in STS, install the JDK in advance.

2.2.1 Install STS

Now let's install STS. Search for "sts download" to display the download site.

[STS Download Site]
  https://spring.io/tools

[STS Download Site]

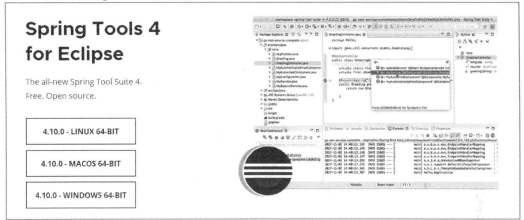

Download the files according to your OS. This book is explained in the Windows version.

Place the downloaded jar file in a path of your choice. Then, in this book, place the jar file directly under the C drive (C:\). Double-click the jar file to create a folder called sts-4.9.0.RELEASE.

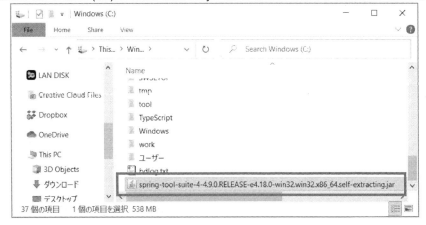

Inside the folder is a file called SpringToolSuite4.exe. This is the eclipse of the STS.

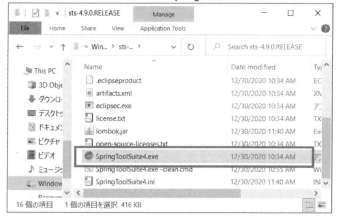

Next, configure the settings in [2.3 Install the Lombok].

2.3 Install the Lombok

Before you create your project, add a useful library called Lombook. Lombok automatically generates non-essential code. For example, methods such as getter and setter are auto-generated. It is very convenient and is used in most development environments. The details of how to use this function are described in Chapter 3 and subsequent chapters. This section describes how to install Lombook.

※The latest eclipse may have Lombok installed.
※Install Lombook with eclipse or STS closed.

First, download the Lombok jar file. You can find the download site by searching for "lombok download".

[Lombok Download Site]
https://projectlombok.org/download

Click Download1.18.XX to download the lombok.jar file.

Double-click the lombok.jar file to launch the installer. Wait for a while and the path of eclipse.exe or SpringToolSuite4.exe will be displayed. If the path does not appear after a while, click Specify. You can specify paths for eclipse.exe and SpringToolSuite4.exe.

Select the exe file on which you want to install Lombok, and press the "Install/Update" button.

If "Install successful" is displayed, the installation is complete.

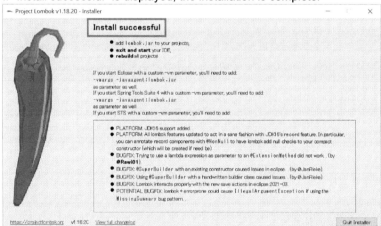

NOTE: eclipse.ini, SpringToolSuite4.ini

If the Lombok does not work correctly, please start eclipse clean or clean the project.

If Lombook still doesn't work, check the contents of eclipse.ini or the SpringToolSuite4.ini file. Make sure that the path for lombok.jar is set in -javaagent.

[eclipse.ini]

-javaagent:C:\pleiades\eclipse\lombok.jar

2.4 Creating a Project

Let's create a SpringBoot project. You must be connected to the Internet to download the library when you create the project.

Right-click Project Explorer > New > Other.

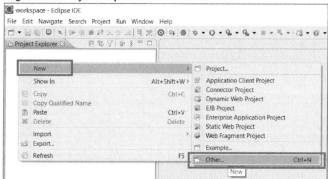

Select Spring Starter Project in SpringBoot.

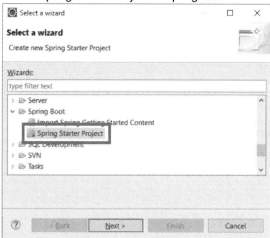

Enter the desired project name in the Name field. In this book, the project name is SpringBootSample.

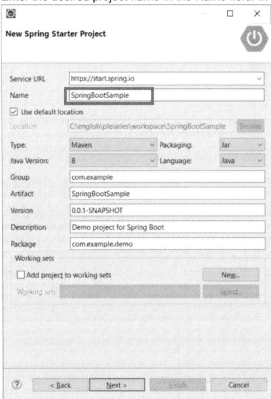

Select the library to be used in the project. After selecting a library, click [Finish]. To download the library, the project is created after a while.

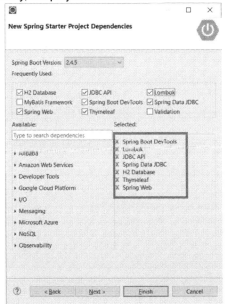

※Depending on the version of SpringBoot, the name of the library may change.

※The latest version of Spring Boot is specified by default. If you want to change the version of Spring Boot, you can change it in a file called pom.xml.

The following libraries are added.

Category	Library
Developer Tools	Spring Boot DevTools
	Lombok
SQL	JDBC API
	Spring Data JDBC
	H2 Database
Template engines	Thymeleaf
Web	Spring Web

NOTE: Selected Library

Provides an overview of each library.

- **Spring Boot DevTools**

  SpringBootDevTools is an auxiliary tool to improve development efficiency. This will automatically restart the web application. For example, suppose you modified and saved your Java code. In this case, the changes do not take effect until the web application is restarted. By installed SpringBootDevTools, you can automatically restart the web application at the moment the file is saved. This reduces reboot operations and improves development efficiency.

- **Lombok**

  You can use your Lombook.

- **JDBC API、Spring Data JDBC**

  Spring allows you to run SQL using JDBC.

- **H2**

  The H2 database does not require setup. Therefore, it can be used as a database for learning and test environments.

- **Thymeleaf**

  Thymeleaf is an HTML template engine used by SpringBoot as standard. The Template Engine is the ability to synthesize HTML templates and data into HTML. For example, a Java list can be looped and displayed as a list.

  Before Thymeleaf was used, JSP was a popular template engine. JSP puts Java code in HTML. As a result, HTML is very unreadable. Thymeleaf improves this point, making HTML much easier to understand.

- **Web**

  You can use SpringMVC to develop web applications.

Note: About Maven

When you create a SpringBoot project, it contains a project management tool called Maven.

Maven manages library dependencies, etc. Libraries may have been created using different libraries. In this case, if Java is not loaded sequentially from the development source library, an error will occur. However, Maven determines their relationships and loads them sequentially. In other words, Maven makes project management easier.

To add, remove, or change the version of a library, edit the file pom.xml. Libraries to be installed in the project are placed in the <dependencies> tag.

[pom.xml]

```
...
<dependencies>
  <dependency>
    <groupId>org.springframework.boot</groupId>
    <artifactId>spring-boot-starter-data-jdbc</artifactId>
  </dependency>
  <dependency>
    <groupId>org.springframework.boot</groupId>
    <artifactId>spring-boot-starter-jdbc</artifactId>
  </dependency>
  <dependency>
    <groupId>org.springframework.boot</groupId>
    <artifactId>spring-boot-starter-thymeleaf</artifactId>
  </dependency>
  <dependency>
    <groupId>org.springframework.boot</groupId>
    <artifactId>spring-boot-starter-web</artifactId>
  </dependency>
  <dependency>
    <groupId>org.springframework.boot</groupId>
    <artifactId>spring-boot-devtools</artifactId>
```

```
        <scope>runtime</scope>
        <optional>true</optional>
    </dependency>
    <dependency>
        <groupId>com.h2database</groupId>
        <artifactId>h2</artifactId>
        <scope>runtime</scope>
    </dependency>
    <dependency>
        <groupId>org.projectlombok</groupId>
        <artifactId>lombok</artifactId>
        <optional>true</optional>
    </dependency>
    <dependency>
        <groupId>org.springframework.boot</groupId>
        <artifactId>spring-boot-starter-test</artifactId>
        <scope>test</scope>
    </dependency>
</dependencies>
...
```

The library you selected earlier and the library SpringBoot installs by default.

These are the libraries required in Chapter 3. The functions required in Chapter 3 and later will be added as needed. Your development environment is now ready. In the following chapters, we will create a simple sample.

3. Hello World...Make a simple sample

This chapter serves two purposes:

- Get used to using Spring Boot
- Get to know the convenience of Spring Boot

To do this, you will create a simple web screen sample. Samples are created in the following order.

- Displaying HTML
- Passing Values from One Screen to Another
- Gets a value from the database

3.1 Displaying HTML

Overview

Create a sample that displays a screen labeled Hello World. The following screen is displayed.

[Sample image]

Hello World

On the server side (Spring Boot), create a class called a controller.

[Overview of Processing]

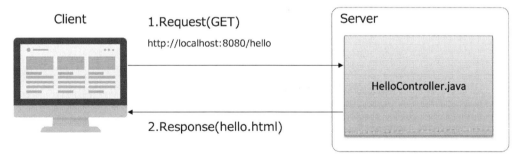

1. **Request (GET method)**
   Enter the URL in your browser to send an HTTP request.
2. **Response (hello.html)**
   When a request to the "http://localhost:8080/hello" is sent to the server, HelloController.java accepts the operation. HelloController.java returns hello.html to the browser.

Note: HTTP GET Methods

When you enter a URL in the browser, the request is sent in the GET method of HTTP. The GET method is used to get data from the server.

Note: What Is a Controller?

A controller is a class that accepts requests.

Directory

The directory structure in the project is as follows. The part where the background color is changed is the new part to be added.

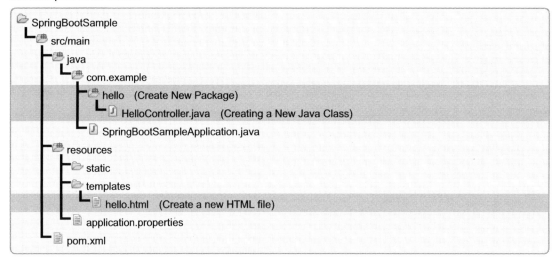

Note: SpringBootSampleApplication.java

When you create a Spring Boot project, a file named "project name + Application.java" is automatically created. This class has the main method. Spring is executed from this main method.

Source Code

Create a new HTML file.
[hello.html]

```
<!DOCTYPE html>
<html xmlns:th="http://www.thymeleaf.org">
<head>
 <meta charset="UTF-8"></meta>
```

```
 <title>Hello World</title>
</head>
<body>
 <h1>Hello World</h1>
</body>
</html>
```

Point: Thymeleaf declaration

Write [xmlns:th="http://www.thymeleaf.org"] in the html tags. You can now use Thymeleaf. The above code does not yet use Thymeleaf. The following example uses Thymeleaf.

Next, create a controller.

[HelloController.java]

```java
package com.example.hello;

import org.springframework.stereotype.Controller;
import org.springframework.web.bind.annotation.GetMapping;

@Controller
public class HelloController {

  @GetMapping("/hello")
  public String getHello() {
    // Screen transition to hello.html
    return "hello";
  }
}
```

Point 1: @Controller

A class that accepts HTTP requests from a screen is called a controller. Classes annotated with @Controller become controllers.

Point 2: @GetMapping

To accept an HTTP request for the GET method, use the @GetMapping annotation. Set the accepted URL to the argument of @GetMapping. For sample code, the GET method now accepts HTTP requests to the "http://localhost:8080/hello".

The return value of the method is the HTML file path without the extension. Specifies a path relative to "src/main/resources/templates" as the return value. For sample code, "src/main/resources/templates/hello.html".

Execution

To run Spring Boot, do the following:

Right-click the project > Run > Spring Boot Application.

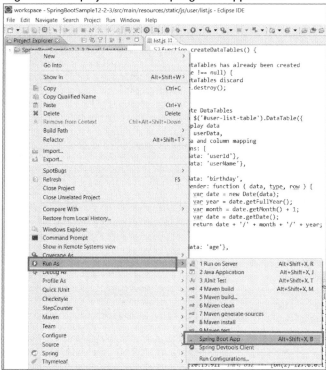

This starts Spring Boot. Then, go to the following URL.

[URL]

http://localhost:8080/hello

[Execution result]

You can now display the screen (HTML).

24

3.2 Passing Values from One Screen to Another

Overview

rom the screen you just created, pass the value to another screen to display it.

[Sample image]

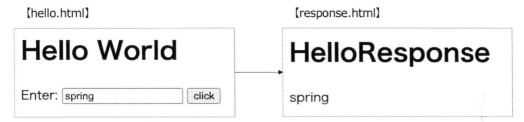

Screen transition from hello.html to response.html. The entered string is displayed in response.html.

[Overview of Processing]

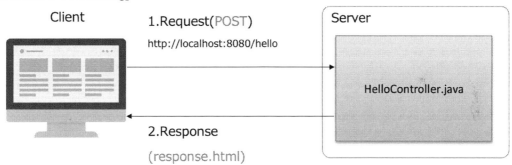

1. **Request (POST method)**
   Use an HTML form to send an HTTP request with the POST method.

2. **Response (response.html)**
   As in the previous example, HelloController.java accepts the operation. If the POST method sends a request, it returns response.html to the browser

Note: HTTP POST Methods

In the html form tag, you can send a request with the HTTP POST method. Use the POST method to ask the server to do something. For example, user registration.

Directory

The directory structure is as follows. The part where the background color is changed is the new part to be added.

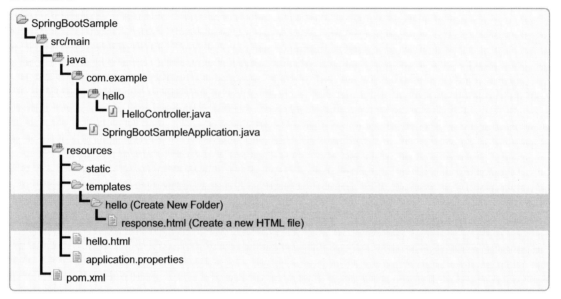

Source Code

First, modify hello.html so that you can enter text. The part where the background color is changed is the modified part.

[hello.html]

```
<!DOCTYPE html>
<html xmlns:th="http://www.thymeleaf.org">
<head>
 <meta charset="UTF-8"></meta>
 <title>Hello World</title>
</head>
<body>
 <h1>Hello World</h1>
 <form method="post" action="/hello">
  Enter: <input type="text" name="text1" />
  <input type="submit" value="click" />
 </form>
</body>
</html>
```

Use the form tag to send a request to the server in the POST method. We have set [name = "text1"] to the input tag.

Then modify the controller to accept POST method requests. The part where the background color is changed is the modified part.

[HelloController.java]

```java
package com.example.hello;

import org.springframework.stereotype.Controller;
import org.springframework.ui.Model;
import org.springframework.web.bind.annotation.GetMapping;
import org.springframework.web.bind.annotation.PostMapping;
import org.springframework.web.bind.annotation.RequestParam;

@Controller
public class HelloController {

    @GetMapping("/hello")
    public String getHello() {
        // Screen transition to hello.html
        return "hello";
    }

    @PostMapping("/hello")
    public String postRequest(@RequestParam("text1") String str, Model model) {
        // Register the string received from the screen to Model
        model.addAttribute("sample", str);

        // Screen transition to response.html
        return "hello/response";
    }
}
```

Point 1: @PostMapping

To receive an HTTP request for the POST method, use the @PostMapping annotation. Set the URL to be accepted in the @PostMapping argument. For sample code, the POST method now accepts HTTP requests to the "http://localhost:8080/hello".

Point 2: @RequestParam

There are several ways the server can receive the values entered on the screen. One of them is to use the @RequestParam annotation. Annotate the method argument with this annotation. Then specify the argument of the @RequestParam annotation to match the HTML name attribute.

In sample code, you specify a string so that the following parts match:

[hello.html]

```html
<input type="text" name="text1" />
```

[HelloController.java]

```
@RequestParam("text1") String str
```

The value entered on the screen is now passed to the str variable.

Point 3: Model class

The Model class allows you to pass values to another screen. Specify the key name and value in the addAttribute method of the Model class.

[addAttribute method]

```
addAttribute(keyname, value);
```

If you register the key and value in the Model class, the screen can receive this value.

Next, create a screen that accepts the entered character string.

[response.html]

```html
<!DOCTYPE html>
<html xmlns:th="http://www.thymeleaf.org">
<head>
  <meta charset="UTF-8"></meta>
  <title>ResponseSample</title>
</head>
<body>
  <h1>HelloResponse</h1>
  <!-- Display the received string -->
  <p th:text="${sample}"></p>
</body>
</html>
```

Point: th attribute

To use Thymeaf, use an attribute with "th:" in HTML. If you enter ${key name} for the value of the "th" attribute, the screen can get the value registered in the Model class.

Execution

Run Spring Boot and access the following URL.

[URL]
http://localhost:8080/hello

[Execution result]

〔hello.html〕   〔response.html〕

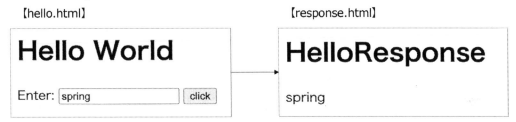

Enter any character string and press the button. The entered character string will be displayed on another screen.

3.3 Gets a value from the database

Overview

Retrieves employee information for the specified ID from the database. Displays information about the employee on the screen.

[Sample image]

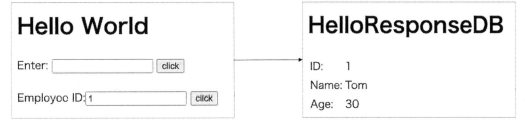

[Overview of Processing]

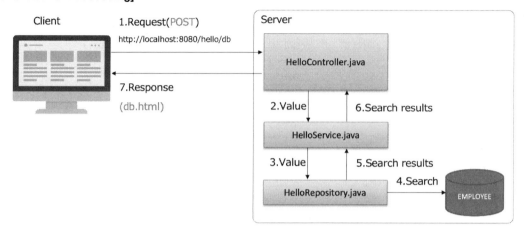

1. Request (POST method)

Use an HTML form to send an HTTP request with the POST method.

2 ~ 3. Value

he controller passes the value entered from the screen to the service, repository.

4. Search

The repository searches the EMPLOYEE table.

5 ~ 6. Search results

The repository, service, returns the search results to the controller.

7. Response

Returns db.html to the browser.

Note: What Is a Service?

Services are classes for various operations. For example, you might want to calculate something or use a repository.

The controller leaves the processing to the service. The service performs all processing. This allows you to reuse the service if you do the same on a different screen.

Note: What is a Repository?

A repository is a class that performs database-related processing.

Directory

The directory structure is as follows. The part where the background color is changed is the new part to be added.

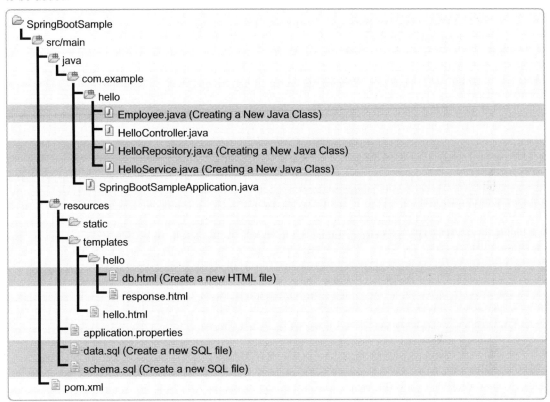

Source Code

Set in application.properties to use the H2 database.
[application.properties]

```
# DataSource
spring.datasource.url=jdbc:h2:mem:testdb;DB_CLOSE_DELAY=-1;DB_CLOSE_ON_EXIT=FALSE
spring.datasource.driver-class-name=org.h2.Driver
spring.datasouce.username=sa
spring.datasouce.password=
spring.datasource.sql-script-encoding=UTF-8
spring.datasource.initialize=true
spring.datasource.schema=classpath:schema.sql
spring.datasource.data=classpath:data.sql

# H2DB
```

```
spring.h2.console.enabled=true
```

Point 1: H2 Database Initialization Settings

The H2 database is an in-memory database. An in-memory database has all its data in memory. Therefore, you can use the database only while Spring Boot is running. Restarting Spring Boot erases the tables and data. Using this mechanism, the H2 database is used for testing, learning, etc.

It is difficult to create a table and populate it each time Spring Boot is started. Therefore, prepare SQL to be executed when Spring Boot is started. Prepare the following SQL:

- Creating tables
- Initial data input

To execute these SQL statements, set the following properties:

- **spring.datasource.initialize**
  Specify true to execute the SQL statements for table creation and data input.
- **spring.datasource.schema**
  It executes the SQL for creating the table.
- **spring.datasource.data**
  SQL statements for initial data input are executed.

The "classpath:" that is set in the property is "src/main/resources".

Prepare SQL for table creation.
[schema.sql]

```
CREATE TABLE IF NOT EXISTS employee (
  id VARCHAR(50) PRIMARY KEY,
  name VARCHAR(50),
  age INT
);
```

Prepare an SQL statement to which initial data is to be input.
[data.sql]

```
INSERT INTO employee (id, name, age)
VALUES('1', 'Tom', 30);
```

Create an Employee class to contain the search results.
[Employee.java]

```
package com.example.hello;

import lombok.Data;
```

```
@Data
public class Employee {
    private String employeeId;
    private String employeeName;
    private int employeeAge;
}
```

Point: @Data annotation

@Data is an annotation provided by Lombok. With this, the following methods are automatically generated.

- getter
- setter
- toString
- hashCode
- equals

This saves you the trouble of re-creating getters and setters even if you rename fields. There are other useful annotations in Lombok.

The next step is to create a process that searches the database for an employee. Use JDBC to execute the select statement.

[HelloRepository.java]

```
package com.example.hello;

import java.util.Map;

import org.springframework.beans.factory.annotation.Autowired;
import org.springframework.jdbc.core.JdbcTemplate;
import org.springframework.stereotype.Repository;

@Repository
public class HelloRepository {

    @Autowired
    private JdbcTemplate jdbcTemplate;

    public Map<String, Object> findById(String id) {
        // SELECT statement
        String query = "SELECT *"
            + " FROM employee"
            + " WHERE id=?";

        // Search execution
        Map<String, Object> employee = jdbcTemplate.queryForMap(query, id);
```

```
      return employee;
  }
}
```

Point 1: @Repository

The repository that represents the DB operation is annotated with @Repository.

Point 2: @Autowired

Annotation for using Dependency Injection. Details will be explained in Chapter 5.

Note: JdbcTemplate

You can use the JDBCTemplate class to execute SQL using JDBC. In the sample of this book, The result of the select statement is put in the Map. The key of this Map contains the column name of the select result. The value of Map contains the value of the select result.

Then create the service. The service uses a repository to get the results of SQL execution.

[HelloService.java]

```java
package com.example.hello;

import java.util.Map;

import org.springframework.beans.factory.annotation.Autowired;
import org.springframework.stereotype.Service;

@Service
public class HelloService {

  @Autowired
  private HelloRepository repository;

  /** Get one employee */
  public Employee getEmployee(String id) {
    // Search
    Map<String, Object> map = repository.findById(id);

    // Get value from Map
    String employeeId = (String) map.get("id");
    String name = (String) map.get("name");
    int age = (Integer) map.get("age");

    // Set the Employee class to a value
    Employee employee = new Employee();
```

```
        employee.setEmployeeId(employeeId);
        employee.setEmployeeName(name);
        employee.setEmployeeAge(age);

        return employee;
    }
}
```

Creating an instance of Employee from the execution result of the select statement.

Then modify the controller. The part where the background color is changed is the modified part.

[HelloController.java]

```
package com.example.hello;

import org.springframework.beans.factory.annotation.Autowired;
import org.springframework.stereotype.Controller;
import org.springframework.ui.Model;
import org.springframework.web.bind.annotation.GetMapping;
import org.springframework.web.bind.annotation.PostMapping;
import org.springframework.web.bind.annotation.RequestParam;

@Controller
public class HelloController {

    @Autowired
    private HelloService service;

    @GetMapping("/hello")
    public String getHello() {
        // Screen transition to hello.html
        return "hello";
    }

    @PostMapping("/hello")
    public String postRequest(@RequestParam("text1") String str, Model model) {
        // Register the string received from the screen to Model
        model.addAttribute("sample", str);

        // Screen transition to response.html
        return "hello/response";
    }

    @PostMapping("/hello/db")
    public String postDbRequest(@RequestParam("text2") String id, Model model) {
        // Search one
        Employee employee = service.getEmployee(id);

        // Save Search Results to Model
        model.addAttribute("employee", employee);
```

```
      // Screen transition to db.html
      return "hello/db";
   }
}
```

The instance of Employee got from the service is registered in Model.

Next, create a screen to display Employee.

[db.html]

```
<!DOCTYPE html>
<html xmlns:th="http://www.thymeleaf.org">
<head>
 <meta charset="UTF-8"></meta>
 <title>ResponseSample</title>
</head>
<body>
 <h1>HelloResponseDB</h1>
 <table>
  <tr>
   <td>ID:</td>
   <td th:text="${employee.employeeId}"></td>
  </tr>
  <tr>
   <td>Name:</td>
   <td th:text="${employee.employeeName}"></td>
  </tr>
  <tr>
   <td>Age:</td>
   <td th:text="${employee.employeeAge}"></td>
  </tr>
 </table>
</body>
</html>
```

If a variable of the class type is registered in Model, specify ${key_name.field_name} in the "th" attribute. You can now retrieve the field values for the Java class.

Finally, modify the screen so that you can enter your employee ID. The part where the background color is changed is the modified part.

[hello.html]

```
<!DOCTYPE html>
<html xmlns:th="http://www.thymeleaf.org">
<head>
 <meta charset="UTF-8"></meta>
 <title>Hello World</title>
</head>
<body>
 <h1>Hello World</h1>
```

```
<form method="post" action="/hello">
  Enter: <input type="text" name="text1" />
  <input type="submit" value="Click" />
</form>
<br/>
<form method="post" action="/hello/db">
  Employee ID:<input type="text" name="text2" th:value="${text2_value}" />
  <input type="submit" value="Click" />
</form>
</body>
</html>
```

Execution

Run Spring Boot. You can then access the H2 database console. Access the console at the following URL:

[H2 Database Console URL]
http://localhost:8080/h2-console

The following screen is displayed.

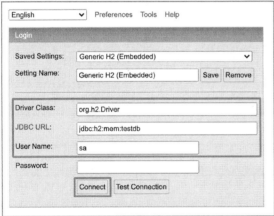

Enter the following information to log in:These values are the values you set in application.properties.

Item	Value	Property
JDBC URL	jdbc:h2:mem:testdb	spring.datasource.url
User Name	sa	spring.datasouce.username

Password	(None)	spring.datasouce.password

When you log in, the following screen is displayed. When you select the EMPLOYEE table, the SQL of the Display All is entered. Click the Execute button to execute the SQL.

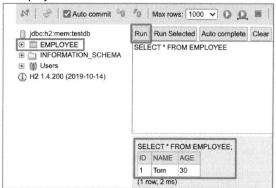

You can confirm that the table is being created and initial data is being entered. You can use the H2 database console to verify test data. Now let's run the sample application. Access the following URL:

[URL]
http://localhost:8080/hello

[Execution result]

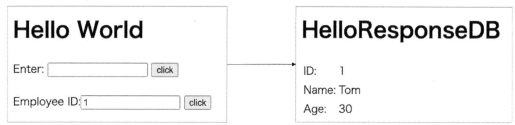

Enter 1 as the employee ID and press the button. The contents registered in the database are displayed on another screen.

This completes the creation of a sample using Spring Boot. This is a simple sample, but we can now see the results of the database search. If you don't use the framework to create these processes, you'll end up with a lot of work.

In the following chapters, we will develop a authentic web application. By doing that, you will learn various ways to use Spring Boot.

4. Web Application Overview

This chapter describes an overview of the applications you create in this book.

Applications that you create now become applications that edit user information. This sounds like a very simple application. However, we will add the functions necessary for the application, such as security and input checking. This allows you to learn a lot about Spring development.

In order to give a concrete image of what kind of application, the following contents will be explained.

- List of screens
- Screen transition diagram
- Screen image

It is OK to think of what kind of thing to make by looking at the screen image.

List of screens

- Login screen
- User signup screen
- User list screen
- User details screen
- Admin authority only screen

Screen transition diagram

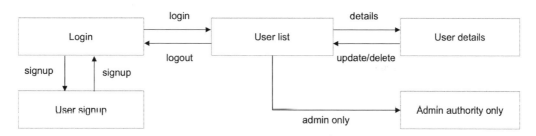

User registration is possible without logging in. Other functions can only be used after logging in.

Screen image

[Login screen]

Create a login feature with Spring security.

[User signup screen]

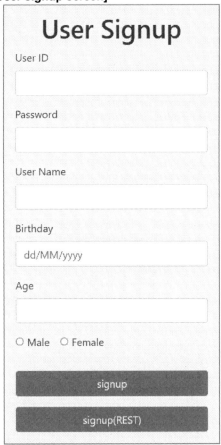

Create a binding and validation (input check). In addition, create a screen so that it can support multiple languages.

[User list screen]

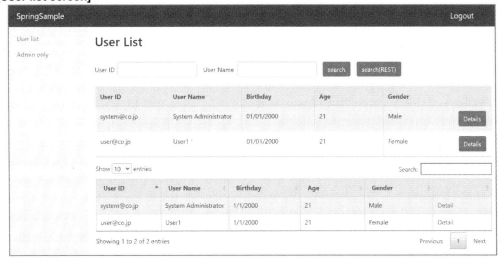

Create a search and list of users. Displays a list of users separately for normal requests and REST requests.

[User details screen]

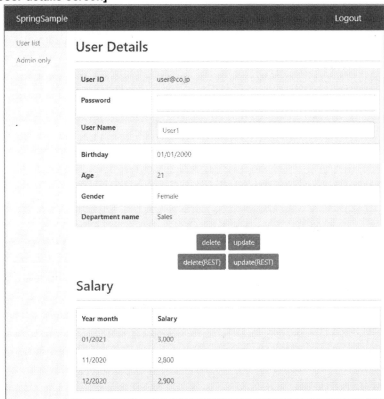

Create a user update/delete function. It also displays the results of table joins.

[Admin authority only screen]

SpringSample	Logout
User list	**Admin authority only screen**
Admin only	

Use permission control in Spring security to create a screen that can only be viewed by users with admin privileges.

As a whole, you will also learn about the following topics:

- Screen layout
- Common error screen
- Database operations with MyBatis and JPA
- REST request function
- Log output by AOP

5. Dependency Injection

The Dependency Injection is referred to as DI for short. DI is also the basis for Spring. In this chapter we will learn about DI. Descriptions are provided in the following order.

- What is DI?
- How to implement DI
- Pitfalls of DI

※ You won't write any code in this chapter, so rest your hands and read.

5.1 What is DI?

Learn what is DI first. DI performs the following two operations.

- Dependency Injection
- Instance Lifecycle Management

5.1.1 Dependency Injection

It's easy to get confused if you suddenly explain dependency injection. Therefore, I will explain DI in the following order in order to take steps.

1. What is dependency?
2. What is injection?
3. What is dependency injection?
4. Why use the interface?
5. What does Spring's DI do?

1. What is dependency?

Dependencies mean that one class has a field in another class or uses a method. For example, the code might look like this:

[Sample code]

```java
public class SomeObjectA {

    // field
    private SomeObjectB objB;

    // constructor
    public SomeObjectA(SomeObjectB objB) {
        this.objB = objB;
    }
}
```

```
// method
public void methodA() {
    objB.methodB();
}
}
```

If you add an argument to a SomeObjectB method, SomeObjectA must modify the code. SomeObjectA relies on SomeObjectB in this case.

2. What is injection?

Next, I will explain what "injection" means. Injection is the assignment of an instance to a variable. In the example code above, the instance is assigned to the field in the constructor.

[Sample code] (Excerpt)

```
// constructor
public SomeObjectA(SomeObjectB objB) {
    this.objB = objB;
}
```

If you do not assign an instance, objB=null will remain. If objB is null, a NullPointerException occurs even if the objB method is called. So, assign the instance with a constructor, setter, etc...

3. What is dependency injection?

If you understand Dependency and Injection, you can easily understand Dependency Injection.

Dependency injection is the assignment of an instance of a class that inherits from an interface or abstract class.

For example, Java has an interface called "List". You cannot assign an instance to it unless it is a class that implements the interface. If you want to inject an "ArrayList" class that implements the "List" interface, write code similar to the following:

```
List<Object> list = new ArrayList<>();
```

An interface or abstract class can have multiple classes that inherit from it. Classes that implement the "List" interface include "ArrayList" and "LinkedList".

If you have more than one implementation class, you need to do two things:

- Which implementation class to use (dependency)
- Insert an instance of the class into a variable (injection)

In other words, decide whether to inject an "ArrayList" or a "LinkedList" into the "List".

The combination of Dependency and Injection results in Dependency Injection.

4. Why use the interface?

Why use interfaces and abstract classes in the first place? The reason is that classes can be exchanged, making them easier to develop and maintain. This has the following advantages:

- Can add or change processing content
- Make testing easier

[Can add or change processing contents]

You can use the interface to change the class. This means that you can change the content of the operation. For example, the contents of "ArrayList" and "LinkedList" that implement List are handled differently. Therefore, there are advantages and disadvantages as follows.

- ArrayList

  - Advantages: Accessing Elements Fast
  - Disadvantages: Element addition is slow

- LinkedList

  - Advantages: Element addition is fast
  - Disadvantages: Slow access to elements

The more you can change the process, the more resistant it is to changes and the more extensible it is. It is easy to switch the implementation class if it is an interface. However, if you use the implementation class as it is, your application will depend only on that class. The code is as follows.

```
// Implementation class can be changed (loosely coupled)
List<Object> listA = new ArrayList<>();
// Cannot be changed to anything other than ArrayList (tightly coupled)
ArrayList<Object> listB = new ArrayList<>();
```

Depending on the implementation class is called tight coupling. The dependency on an interface is called loosely coupled. The class diagram looks like this:

[Tight coupled]   **[Loosely coupled]**

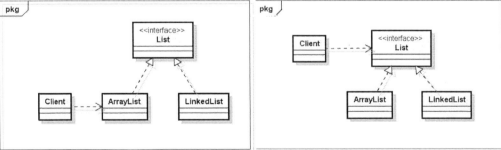

You can see that loosely coupled is dependent on "List". Therefore, it can be changed to either

"ArrayList" or "LinkedList". Alternatively, you can add a new class that implements "List".

[Make testing easier]

If you can change the class, you can prepare stubs for easy testing. A stub is a class that has written dummy processing. For example, suppose you create a mail-sending feature. Prepare a stub that logs the contents of the email without sending the email. This way, you can develop and test the process before and after sending mail, even if the mail cannot be sent.

Also suppose you find a bug and fixed the code a bit. It's hard to manually redo the test, even though you've only modified the code a bit. Some people skip testing what seems irrelevant. If you write test code at such times, you can automate the test. Stubs are needed to automate testing.

Preparing an interface makes testing easier. This makes development and maintenance easier.

5. What does Spring's DI do?

Now that you understand dependency injection, then explain what Spring DI is doing. DI performs the following processing.

1. Look for the DI's target class
2. Injecting instances where they are annotated with @Autowired

I will explain it in order.

1. Look for the DI's target class

When Spring starts, it looks for the class that is the target of DI. This process is called component scan. The component scan looks for the following annotated classes:

[DI target annotation]

- @Component
- @Controller
- @Service
- @Repository
- @Configuration
- @RestController
- @ControllerAdvice
- @ManagedBean
- @Named
- @Mapper
- @Bean

The class with these annotations is then registered in the DI container. A DI container is a container that manages DI target classes.

For example, suppose you have one class each annotated with "@Controller" and "@Service". In that case, please think DI container is created as follows. It's just an imaginary code to make it easier to understand.

[DI Container Image]

```
public class DIContainer {

    // Create an instance of each class
    private SampleController controller = new SampleController();
    private SampleService service = new SampleService();

    // SampleController getter
    public static SampleController getSampleController() {
        return controller;
    }

    // SampleService getter
    public static SampleService getSampleService() {
        return service;
    }
}
```

It has an instance of each class as a field. Think of it as creating a class with those getters.

A class registered in a DI container is called a "bean". In the example code above, both SampleController and SampleService are beans.

2. Injecting instances where they are annotated with @Autowired

Then inject the instance where it is annotated with @Autowired. Imagine the code being converted as follows:

[Before conversion]

```
@Autowired
private SampleService service;
```

[After conversion]

```
private SampleService service = DIContainer.getSampleService()
```

As mentioned above, the instance is injected where @Autowired is attached.
※ It's just an imaginary code to make it easier to understand.

Why is DI doing this? You might have thought. The answer lies in the reason for using the interface. Using the interface provided the following benefits:

- Can add or change processing contents
- Make testing easier

By using DI, you can dynamically change the class that implements the interface. For example, use stubs for testing. At other times, use the production class. If you write dependency injection directly in your code, you'll have to modify your code to change the class.

[Bad Example Sample Code]

```
@Controller
public class SampleController {
  // Injecting instances directly in code (NG)
  private SampleService service = new SampleServiceImpl();

  @PostMapping("/sample")
  public String postSample() {
    // Some processing using service
    ...
  }
}
```

This prevents you from changing SampleService to a stub during testing. In addition, even if you create a new class, it becomes difficult to switch to that class.

Using DI, you can easily change the implementation class.

5.1.2 Instance Lifecycle Management

DI also provides lifecycle management for instances. In particular, it creates and destroys instances.

Creating an instance means assigning a new instance to a variable. Destroying an instance means assigning null to a variable. If you assign null to a variable, the garbage collection frees the instance from memory. In particular, the following code creates and destroys instances:

[Sample code]

```
// Creating an Instance
SomeObject obj = new SomeObject()
// Destroying an instance
obj = null
```

Spring's DI automatically creates and destroys instances. Their timing can be specified by scope. Scope is the amount of time an instance lives. For example, the request scope creates an instance each time an HTTP request is sent. The instance is then destroyed when the request is finished processing.

To specify a scope, annotate the class with @Scope.

[Sample code for scope specification]

```
@Controller
@Scope("request")
public class SomeController {
  ...
}
```

Spring provides the following scopes:

[Scope List]

Scope	Description
singleton	Spring creates only one instance at startup. One instance is shared and used throughout the application. **Without the @Scope annotation, all are singletons.**
prototype	Each time you get a bean, an instance is created.
session	Instances are created per HTTP session. That is, the instance exists only while the user is logged in. Available only for web applications.
request	An instance is created for each HTTP request. Available only for web applications.
globalSession	Instances are created per GrobalSession in the portlet environment. Available only for web applications that support portlets.
application	Instances are created per servlet context. Available only for web applications.

5.2 How to implement DI

Now you'll learn how to implement DI.

- Dependency Injection Methods
- How to register a bean

5.2.1 Dependency Injection Methods

To use DI, use the @Autowired annotation. I will explain how to use it. The @Autowired annotation can be used in three places:

1. Field
2. Constructors
3. Setter

1. Field Injection

The way to inject dependencies into a field is to annotate the field with @Autowired.

[Sample code]

```
@Component
public class Sample {
  // Field injection
  @Autowired
  private SampleComponent component;
}
```

2. Constructor Injection

Dependencies can be injected into constructor arguments. Note that in Spring 4.3 and later, you can omit the @Autowired annotation of the constructor injection.

[Sample code]

```
@Component
public class Sample {

  private final SampleComponent component;

  // Constructor Injection
  @Autowired
  public Sample(SampleComponent component) {
    this.component = component;
  }
}
```

Spring recommends constructor injection.

You can also use Lombook to automatically generate constructors.

[Lombok Sample Code 1]

```
@Component
@RequiredArgsConstructor
public class Sample {
  private final SampleComponent component;
  private String value;
}
```

Point: @RequiredArgsConstructor

The @RequiredArgsConstructor annotation creates a constructor that takes only fields with the final modifier as arguments. In the example code above, a constructor is created with only the arguments of SampleComponent.

[Lombok Sample Code 2]

```
@Component
@AllArgsConstructor
public class Sample {
    private SampleComponent component;
    private String value;
}
```

Point: @AllArgsConstructor

The @AllArgsConstructor annotation creates a constructor with all fields as arguments.

You can omit @Autowired in constructor injection. Therefore, DI is executed with the above sample code.

3. Setter Injection

You can inject dependencies into the arguments of setter. Annotate setter with @Autowired.
[Sample code]

```
@Component
public class Sample {

    private SampleComponent component;

    // setter injection
    @Autowired
    public void setComponent(SampleComponent component) {
        this.component = component;
    }
}
```

5.2.2 How to register a bean

A class registered in a DI container is called a bean. There are several ways to create a bean, but the main way is to use a combination of the following two:

1. Annotation-based implementation
2. Implementation in JavaConfig

1. Annotation-based implementation

To use DI, annotate the class with the @Controller and other annotations used in the example code in Chapter 3. Among other things, the following annotations are commonly used:

- @Component
- @Controller
- @Service
- @Repository
- @Bean
- @Mapper

It is fundamental to register a bean in a DI container by annotating the class.

2. Implementation in JavaConfig

The class that instantiates a bean is commonly referred to as JavaConfig. Use JavaConfig in situations such as when bean generation is complex. For example, to register a class provided in a library in a DI container.

[Sample code]

```
@Configuration
public class JavaConfig {

    @Bean
    public SomeComponent getSomeComponent() {
        return new SomeComponentImpl();
    }
}
```

Point: @Configuration, @Bean

Annotate JavaConfig classes with @Configuration.

Then annotate the method that creates the instance with @Bean. You can add @Scope annotation along with @Bean annotation.

It is difficult to register all classes as beans with JavaConfig. Therefore, basically, "annotation-based implementation" is used. If that is not enough, you will also use "Implementation in JavaConfig".

5.3 Pitfalls of DI

Although DI is useful, it has the following pitfalls:

- Singleton Scope
- Different scopes
- Cannot be DI from other than Bean

5.3.1 Singleton Scope

Annotations such as @Service default to singleton scope. There is only one instance of singleton during application startup. Two or more instances are not created. Therefore, be careful when accessing from multiple instances. In such cases, don't write code like this:

[Bad example sample code]

```java
@Getter
@Setter
@Service
public class SomeServiceImpl implements SomeService {

    // Some state
    private String state;

    @Override
    public void someMethod() {
        // Some processing using state
        ...
    }
}
```

The above services are supposed to be used as follows.

1. Set the state field to some value.
2. Do some processing using state with someMethod.

What's wrong with the above code is that another instance can rewrite the state. Suppose the state is rewritten while calling processes 1 and 2. In that case, someMethod returns an unexpected execution result.

There are several workarounds for this. For example, changing a field to a method argument.

[Good example sample code]

```java
@Service
public class SomeServiceImpl implements SomeService {

    @Override
    public void someMethod(String state) {
        // Some processing using state
```

```
    ...
  }
}
```

In this way, classes with no state are called stateless classes.

Another solution is to use a scope other than singleton.

5.3.2 Different scopes

Instances may not be destroyed if the fields have different scopes. This is a pitfall of the Java specification. For example, if an instance of singleton scope has an instance of prototype scope in a field.

[Bad example sample code]

```
@Component
@Scope("prototype")
public class PrototypeComponent {
    ...
}
```

[Bad example sample code]

```
@Component
public class SingletonComponent {
    @Autowired
    private PrototypeComponent component;
    ...
}
```

If you do this, the Bean with the prototype scope (PrototypeComponent above) will become the singleton scope. The same thing happens if you have a bean with request scope set in a bean with session scope.

Be careful when having beans with different scopes as fields.

5.3.3 Cannot be DI from other than Bean

It's easy to overlook, but you can't do DI from non-bean classes.

[Bad example sample code]

```
public class SampleObject {
```

```
    @Autowired
    private SampleService service;

    ...
}
```

In the example code above, the SampleObject is not annotated with @Component or @Controller. That is, a SampleObject is not a bean. This does not allow DI in the SampleService field.

Annotate the class as follows:

[Good example sample code]

```
@Component
public class SampleObject {

    @Autowired
    private SampleService service;

    ...
}
```

Summary

Here's what you've learned in this chapter.

[What is DI?]

DI does the following:

- Automatically assigns an instance to an interface.
- Instances are created and destroyed.
- You can manage the scope of an instance.

[How to implement DI]

You can annotate @Autowired in three places:

- Field
- Constructors
- Setter

In order to implement DI, it is mainstream to combine the following two methods.

- Annotation-based implementation
- Implementation in JavaConfig

[Pitfalls of DI]

DI has the following pitfalls:

- Singleton scope.
- If you have beans in different scopes in the field, the instance will not be destroyed.
- DI cannot be executed from other than Bean.

6. Bind and Validation (Input Check)

In this chapter, you will learn about binding and validation (input checking) as you create your screen. Both are fundamental to screen creation, so you need to be familiar with them.

- Create Screen
- Data Binding
- Validation (input check)

6.1 Create Screen

Learn about creating screens with Spring Boot.

- Using Libraries...webjars
- Message Properties
- Multilingualization

6.1.1 Using Libraries...webjars

Overview

Screen design is becoming more important in applications. The Bootstrap framework is often used when designing screens. Bootstrap makes it easy to create beautiful screens. You can also create screens that are compatible with smartphones.

To use Bootstrap, you use a library called webjars. Webjars makes it easy to download and load libraries. In this section, you will create the following two screens.

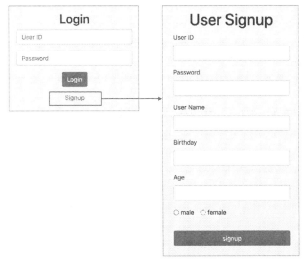

Directory

The directory structure is as follows. The part where the background color is changed is the modified part.

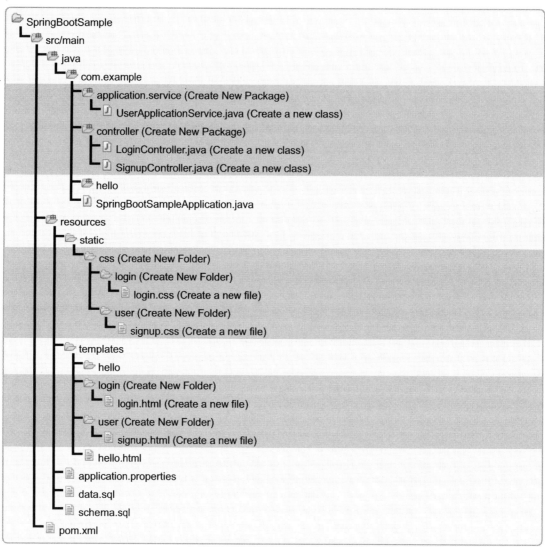

Source Code

First, make webjars available. Edit pom.xml to do so. Add the following code in the dependencies tag of pom.xml. The part where the background color is changed is the added part.

[pom.xml]

```xml
<dependencies>
...
<!-- jquery -->
<dependency>
  <groupId>org.webjars</groupId>
  <artifactId>jquery</artifactId>
  <version>3.5.1</version>
</dependency>
<!-- bootstrap -->
<dependency>
  <groupId>org.webjars</groupId>
  <artifactId>bootstrap</artifactId>
  <version>4.5.3</version>
</dependency>
<!-- webjars-locator -->
<dependency>
  <groupId>org.webjars</groupId>
  <artifactId>webjars-locator</artifactId>
  <version>0.40</version>
</dependency>
...
</dependencies>
```

Point 1: What is webjars?

Webjars are libraries that make libraries such as JavaScript and CSS available to Maven. See the official webjars page. You can find the libraries provided by webjars by searching for "maven webjars".

Point 2: What is webjars-locator?

Webjars-locator allows you to write code without being aware of the version of the library used by webjars. The details of how to use this function will be explained later.

Note: jQuery

To use Bootstrap, you need a JavaScript library called jQuery.

Edit pom.xml and Maven will automatically download the library.

On the user signup screen, a radio button for selecting gender is displayed. Create a service that generates a gender map.

[UserApplicationService.java]

```java
package com.example.application.service;
```

```
import java.util.LinkedHashMap;
import java.util.Map;

import org.springframework.stereotype.Service;

@Service
public class UserApplicationService {

  /** Generate a gender Map */
  public Map<String, Integer> getGenderMap() {
    Map<String, Integer> genderMap = new LinkedHashMap<>();
    genderMap.put("male", 1);
    genderMap.put("female", 2);
    return genderMap;
  }
}
```

Next, create a controller for the login screen.

[LoginController.java.java]

```
package com.example.controller;

import org.springframework.stereotype.Controller;
import org.springframework.web.bind.annotation.GetMapping;

@Controller
public class LoginController {

  /** Display login screen */
  @GetMapping("/login")
  public String getLogin() {
    return "login/login";
  }
}
```

Next, create a controller for the user signup screen.

[SignupController.java]

```
package com.example.controller;

import java.util.Map;

import org.springframework.beans.factory.annotation.Autowired;
import org.springframework.stereotype.Controller;
import org.springframework.ui.Model;
import org.springframework.web.bind.annotation.GetMapping;
import org.springframework.web.bind.annotation.PostMapping;
import org.springframework.web.bind.annotation.RequestMapping;
```

```
import com.example.application.service.UserApplicationService;

@Controller
@RequestMapping("/user")
public class SignupController {

    @Autowired
    private UserApplicationService userApplicationService;

    /** Display the user signup screen */
    @GetMapping("/signup")
    public String getSignup(Model model) {
        // Get gender
        Map<String, Integer> genderMap = userApplicationService.getGenderMap();
        model.addAttribute("genderMap", genderMap);

        // Transition to user signup screen
        return "user/signup";
    }

    /** User signup process */
    @PostMapping("/signup")
    public String postSignup() {
        // Redirect to login screen
        return "redirect:/login";
    }
}
```

Point: @RequestMapping

When @RequestMapping is added to a class, it can be used as a URL prefix.

In the sample code above, the settings are as follows.

- Class: @RequestMapping("/user")
- Method: @GetMapping("/signup")

To access the user signup screen with this setting, enter the following URL.

[URL of the user signup screen]

http://localhost:8080/user/signup

You can also add @RequestMapping to a method instead of @GetMapping or @PostMapping.

[Sample] Substitute for @GetMapping

```
@RequestMapping(value = "/sample", method=RequestMethod.GET)
public String getSample() {
    ...
}
```

Note: Redirection

To redirect, specify "redirect: Redirect destination path" as the return value.

Note: PRG Pattern

The PRG pattern is a screen transition by redirect after executing the POST method. When redirecting, get the next screen with the GET method. The acronym for POST-Redirect-GET is called the PRG pattern. Use the PRG pattern to prevent accidental registration or renewal.

[When not using PRG pattern]

Suppose you have an application that transitions to the screen without redirecting after registering something. Immediately after the registration operation, press the F5 key on the browser (for Windows). Then the same request will be sent and the registration process will be performed again.

[When using PRG pattern]

If you make a redirect after performing registration or other processing, the request will not be sent even if you press the F5 key. This prevents accidental operation by the user.

Next, create HTML for the login screen.

[login.html]

```html
<!DOCTYPE html>
<html xmlns:th="http://www.thymeleaf.org">
<head>
 <meta charset="UTF-8"></meta>
 <meta name="viewport" content="width=device-width, initial-scale=1, shrink-to-fit=no">
 <!-- Read CSS -->
 <link rel="stylesheet" th:href="@{/webjars/bootstrap/css/bootstrap.min.css}">
 <link rel="stylesheet" th:href="@{/css/login/login.css}">
 <!-- Read JS -->
 <script th:src="@{/webjars/jquery/jquery.min.js}" defer></script>
 <script th:src="@{/webjars/bootstrap/js/bootstrap.min.js}" defer></script>
 <title>Login</title>
</head>
<body class="bg-light">
 <div class="text-center">
  <form method="post" th:action="@{/login}" class="form-login">
   <h2>Login</h2>
   <!-- User ID -->
   <div class="form-group">
    <label for="userId" class="sr-only">userId</label>
    <input type="text" class="form-control" placeholder="User ID"
      name="userId"/>
   </div>
   <!-- Password -->
   <div class="form-group">
```

```
      <label for="password" class="sr-only">password</label>
      <input type="text" class="form-control" placeholder="Password"
        name="password"/>
    </div>
    <input type="submit" value="Login" class="btn btn-primary" />
  </form>
  <a th:href="@{/user/signup}">Signup</a>
 </div>
</body>
</html>
```

Point: Calling webjars

Libraries downloaded with webjars can be loaded with @ {/ webjars /...}. If you look inside the "Maven Dependencies" folder, you will find the jar file of the library downloaded by Maven. From these, check the library specified by webjars.

[Maven dependency folder] (jQuery-3.5.1.jar)

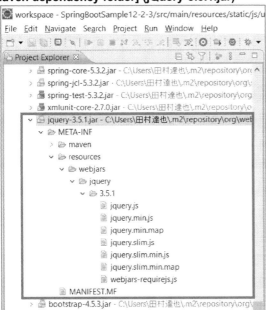

For the path specified in @ {/ webjars /...}, specify the path under "META-INF / resources". Note that the folder with the version number must also be included in the path. For example, to read a jQuery file with the sample code above, you need to write the following code.

[Sample] Path specification including the version number

```
<script th:src="@{/webjars/jquery/3.5.1/jquery.min.js}" defer></script>
```

However, you can omit the version number by including webjars-locator. This saves you the trouble of changing the code even if you change the version of the library that webjars uses.

In other words, webjars and webjars-locator save you the trouble of managing libraries.

Note: JavaScript Performance Measures

When loading JavaScript, add the "defer" attribute. This is because adding the defer attribute improves the screen display performance.

If you add the defer attribute, HTML and JavaScript will be loaded in parallel. If you do not add the defer attribute, the file will not be read in parallel, so the process will be slow.

Note: input type="password"

You must use [input type = "password"] in the password entry field. This book uses [input type = "text"] to display the password entered on the screen.

Next, create HTML for the user signup screen.

[signup.html]

```
<!DOCTYPE html>
<html xmlns:th="http://www.thymeleaf.org">
<head>
 <meta charset="UTF-8"></meta>
 <meta name="viewport" content="width=device-width, initial-scale=1, shrink-to-fit=no">
 <!-- Read CSS -->
 <link rel="stylesheet" th:href="@{/webjars/bootstrap/css/bootstrap.min.css}">
 <link rel="stylesheet" th:href="@{/css/user/signup.css}">
 <!-- Read JS -->
 <script th:src="@{/webjars/jquery/jquery.min.js}" defer></script>
 <script th:src="@{/webjars/bootstrap/js/bootstrap.min.js}" defer></script>
 <title>User Signup</title>
</head>
<body class="bg-light">
 <form id="signup-form" method="post" action="/user/signup"
   class="form-signup">
  <h1 class="text-center">User Signup</h1>
  <!-- User ID -->
  <div class="form-group">
   <label for="userId">User ID</label>
   <input type="text" class="form-control"/>
  </div>
  <!-- Password -->
  <div class="form-group">
   <label for="password">Password</label>
   <input type="text" class="form-control"/>
  </div>
  <!-- User Name -->
  <div class="form-group">
```

```
        <label for="userName">User Name</label>
        <input type="text" class="form-control"/>
    </div>
    <!-- Birthday -->
    <div class="form-group">
        <label for="birthday">Birthday</label>
        <input type="text" class="form-control"/>
    </div>
    <!-- Age -->
    <div class="form-group">
        <label for="age">Age</label>
        <input type="text" class="form-control"/>
    </div>
    <!-- Gender -->
    <div class="form-group">
        <div th:each="item : ${genderMap}" class="form-check-inline">
            <input type="radio" class="form-check-input" th:value="${item.value}"/>
            <label class="form-check-label" th:text="${item.key}"></label>
        </div>
    </div>
    <!-- Signup button -->
    <input type="submit" value="signup"
        class="btn btn-primary w-100 mt-3" />
</form>
</body>
</html>
```

Next, create a CSS for the login screen.

[login.css]

```css
.form-login {
    width: 100%;
    max-width: 330px;
    padding: 15px;
    margin: auto;
}
```

Finally, create a CSS for the user signup screen.

[signup.css]

```css
.form-signup {
    width: 100%;
    max-width: 330px;
    padding: 15px;
    margin: auto;
}
```

Execution

Run Spring Boot and access the following URL.

[URL]
http://localhost:8080/login

[Execution result]

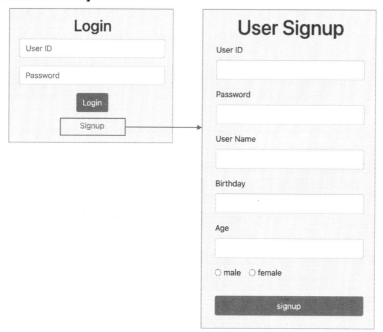

Click the link of "signup" to move to the user signup screen. This completes the screen creation.

6.1.2 Message Properties

Overview

The HTML file you just created contains fixed string, such as "User ID". Here you modify the code to read a fixed string from the property file. In this way, you can edit the properties file to change all the fixed string at once. By doing this, you can change the fixed string at once by simply editing the property file.

In addition to fixed string, messages such as "Signup completed" can be managed in the property file. This has the following advantages.

- **Can standardize and manage screens**
  If the messages displayed on each screen are disparate, the burden is high for the user. By collectively managing messages, the screen is easy for users to understand.

- **Can be multilingualized**
  For applications used overseas, you need to change the language displayed on the screen. By preparing a property file, you can easily switch languages. Multilingualization is explained in [6.1.3 Multilingualization].

Modify the fixed string on the user signup screen so that it is read from the property file.

Directory

The directory structure is as follows. The part where the background color is changed is the new part to be added.

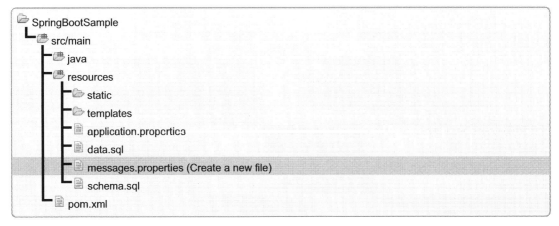

Source Code

In messages.properties, set the string to display on the screen. Set properties in the form "key = value".

[messages.properties]

```
user.signup.title=User Signup
user.signup.btn=signup
userId=User ID
password=Password
userName=User Name
birthday=Birthday
age=Age
male=Male
female=Female
```

Modify the HTML to read the values that you set in messages.properties. The part where the background color is changed is the modified part.

[signup.html]

```
<!DOCTYPE html>
<html xmlns:th="http://www.thymeleaf.org">
<head>
  <meta charset="UTF-8"></meta>
  <meta name="viewport" content="width=device-width, initial-scale=1, shrink-to-fit=no">
  <!-- Read CSS -->
  <link rel="stylesheet" th:href="@{/webjars/bootstrap/css/bootstrap.min.css}">
  <link rel="stylesheet" th:href="@{/css/user/signup.css}">
  <!-- Read JS -->
  <script th:src="@{/webjars/jquery/jquery.min.js}" defer></script>
  <script th:src="@{/webjars/bootstrap/js/bootstrap.min.js}" defer></script>
  <title th:text="#{user.signup.title}"></title>
</head>
<body class="bg-light">
  <form id="signup-form" method="post" action="/user/signup"
    class="form-signup">
    <h1 class="text-center" th:text="#{user.signup.title}"></h1>
    <!-- User ID -->
    <div class="form-group">
      <label for="userId" th:text="#{userId}"></label>
      <input type="text" class="form-control"/>
    </div>
    <!-- Password -->
    <div class="form-group">
      <label for="password" th:text="#{password}"></label>
      <input type="text" class="form-control"/>
    </div>
    <!-- User Name -->
    <div class="form-group">
```

```html
          <label for="userName" th:text="#{userName}"></label>
          <input type="text" class="form-control"/>
        </div>
        <!-- Birthday -->
        <div class="form-group">
          <label for="birthday" th:text="#{birthday}"></label>
          <input type="text" class="form-control"/>
        </div>
        <!-- Age -->
        <div class="form-group">
          <label for="age" th:text="#{age}"></label>
          <input type="text" class="form-control"/>
        </div>
        <!-- Gender -->
        <div class="form-group">
          <div th:each="item : ${genderMap}" class="form-check-inline">
            <input type="radio" class="form-check-input" th:value="${item.value}"/>
            <label class="form-check-label" th:text="${item.key}"></label>
          </div>
        </div>
        <!-- Signup button -->
        <input type="submit" th:value="#{user.signup.btn}"
            class="btn btn-primary w-100 mt-3" />
      </form>
    </body>
</html>
```

Point: Get values from messages.properties

To display the values retrieved from messages.properties, specify #{key name} as the value for the th attribute. This retrieves the value of the appropriate key from messages.properties.

The string displayed on the radio button for the gender was set by the service. Modify the service to get the string from messages.properties. The part where the background color is changed is the modified part.

[UserApplicationService.java]

```java
package com.example.application.service;

import java.util.LinkedHashMap;
import java.util.Locale;
import java.util.Map;

import org.springframework.beans.factory.annotation.Autowired;
import org.springframework.context.MessageSource;
import org.springframework.stereotype.Service;

@Service
public class UserApplicationService {
```

```
@Autowired
private MessageSource messageSource;

/** Generate a gender Map */
public Map<String, Integer> getGenderMap() {
    Map<String, Integer> genderMap = new LinkedHashMap<>();
    String male = messageSource.getMessage("male", null, Locale.ENGLISH);
    String female = messageSource.getMessage("female", null, Locale.ENGLISH);
    genderMap.put(male, 1);
    genderMap.put(female, 2);
    return genderMap;
}
}
```

Point: MessageSource

To get values from messages.properties, use MessageSource. You can use the getMessage method of MessageSource to get the value of messages.properties.

[getMessage method]

getMessage(key name, embedded parameter, locale)

Argument	Description
key name	Specify the key name for messages.properties.
embedded parameter	Allows you to specify the parameters to be included in the message.
locale	Specify the country (region).

If you use MessageSource, you can also get the message when registration is completed.

Execution

Run Spring Boot and access the following URL.

[URL]
http://localhost:8080/user/signup

[Execution result]

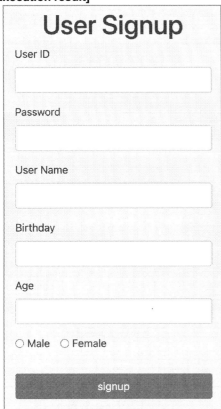

If string are displayed, the values are being read from messages.properties.

Spring Boot Primer Second Edition

6.1.3 Multilingualization

Overview

Modify the application so that you can switch between the languages displayed on the screen. Prepare a properties file for German.

[User signup screen] (German)

Anmeldung

Benutzer-ID

Passwort

Benutzername

Geburtstag

dd/MM/yyyy

Alter

○ Männlich ○ Weiblich

anmeldung

Directory

The directory structure is as follows. The part where the background color is changed is the new part to be added.

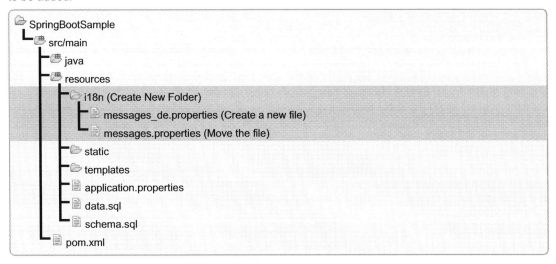

※**Move the messages.properties file under "src/main/resources/i18n".**

Source Code

The path to the messages.properties file defaults to src/main/resources. Edit application.properties to modify the path to the messages.properties file. The part where the background color is changed is the modified part.

[application.properties]

```
# DataSource
spring.datasource.url=jdbc:h2:mem:testdb;DB_CLOSE_DELAY=-1;DB_CLOSE_ON_EXIT=FALSE
spring.datasource.driver-class-name=org.h2.Driver
spring.datasouce.username=sa
spring.datasouce.password=
spring.datasource.sql-script-encoding=UTF-8
spring.datasource.initialize=true
spring.datasource.schema=classpath:schema.sql
spring.datasource.data=classpath:data.sql

# H2DB
spring.h2.console.enabled=true

# message
spring.messages.basename=i18n/messages
```

Point:spring.messages.basename

spring.messages.basename is set to a path relative to src/main/resources. Note that the value does not have a file extension. This is because the file name to be read changes for each language. Give your files names, such as messages_de.properties for German, messages_fr.properties for French, and so on.

Create a German message file. You have to prepare the same key as messages.properties.

[messages_de.properties]

```
user.signup.title=Anmeldung
user.signup.btn=anmeldung
userId=Benutzer-ID
password=Passwort
userName=Benutzername
birthday=Geburtstag
age=Alter
male=Männlich
female=Weiblich
```

Modify the part that we are using the MessageSource. The part where the background color is changed is the modified part.

[UserApplicationService.java]

```java
@Service
public class UserApplicationService {

    @Autowired
    private MessageSource messageSource;

    /** Generate a gender Map */
    public Map<String, Integer> getGenderMap(Locale locale) {
        Map<String, Integer> genderMap = new LinkedHashMap<>();
        String male = messageSource.getMessage("male", null, locale);
        String female = messageSource.getMessage("female", null, locale);
        genderMap.put(male, 1);
        genderMap.put(female, 2);
        return genderMap;
    }
}
```

Accepts a Locale as an argument to a method. The modification is to pass the Locale to the method of the MessageSource.

Modify the user signup controller to receive Locale. The part where the background color is changed is the modified part.

[SignupController.java]

```java
package com.example.controller;

import java.util.Locale;
import java.util.Map;

import org.springframework.beans.factory.annotation.Autowired;
import org.springframework.stereotype.Controller;
import org.springframework.ui.Model;
import org.springframework.web.bind.annotation.GetMapping;
import org.springframework.web.bind.annotation.PostMapping;
import org.springframework.web.bind.annotation.RequestMapping;

import com.example.application.service.UserApplicationService;

@Controller
@RequestMapping("/user")
public class SignupController {

    @Autowired
    private UserApplicationService userApplicationService;

    /** Display the user signup screen */
    @GetMapping("/signup")
    public String getSignup(Model model, Locale locale) {
        // Get gender
        Map<String, Integer> genderMap = userApplicationService.getGenderMap(locale);
        model.addAttribute("genderMap", genderMap);

        // Transition to user signup screen
        return "user/signup";
    }

    /** User signup process */
    @PostMapping("/signup")
    public String postSignup() {
        // Redirect to login screen
        return "redirect:/login";
    }
}
```

Note: About Controller Class Method Arguments

In the method argument of the controller class, you can set the value of various classes such as the value passed from the screen.

Execution

Change the browser language setting. This book explains on the Google Chrome screen. Open the settings from the upper right corner of the chrome.

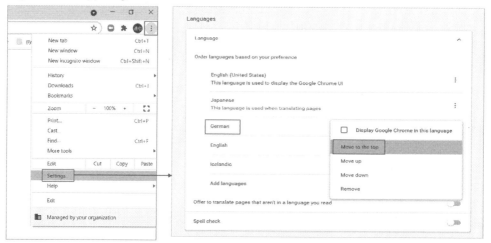

Open Advanced Settings and move German to the top. Run Spring Boot and access the following URL.

[URL]

http://localhost:8080/user/signup

[Execution result]

If the screen appears in German, multilingualization is complete. Set the language back to English.

6.2 Data Binding

Once you've created a screen, you'll learn more about binding.

- Binding
- Edit error messages

6.2.1 Binding

Overview

Binding is the mapping of screen inputs to Java classes. The following is an example of the user signup screen.

[Binding Image]

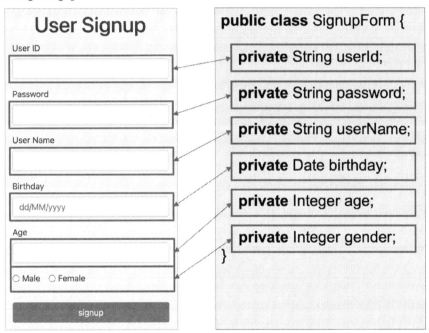

By binding, the input contents of the screen can be received by the controller class on the server side.

Directory

The directory structure is as follows. The part where the background color is changed is the new part to be added.

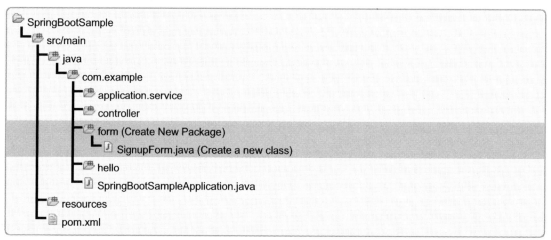

Source Code

First, prepare a form class that maps to the input contents of the screen.

[SignupForm.java]

```java
package com.example.form;

import java.util.Date;

import org.springframework.format.annotation.DateTimeFormat;

import lombok.Data;

@Data
public class SignupForm {
    private String userId;
    private String password;
    private String userName;
    @DateTimeFormat(pattern = "dd/MM/yyyy")
    private Date birthday;
    private Integer age;
    private Integer gender;
}
```

Point: @DateTimeFormat

When binding to a Date type, use the @DateTimeFormat annotation. If entered in the format set for the "pattern" attribute, it can be bound to a Date type.

Note: @NumberFormat

To convert a string in the specified format to a numeric type, use the @NumberFormat annotation.

[Sample]

```
@NumberFormat(pattern = "#,###")
private Integer salary;
```

You can use the code above to convert a comma delimiter, such as 1,000,000, to a numeric type.

Next, modify the user-signup controller so that you can interact with the screen and form instances. The part where the background color is changed is the modified part.

[SignupController.java]

```
package com.example.controller;

import java.util.Locale;
import java.util.Map;

import org.springframework.beans.factory.annotation.Autowired;
import org.springframework.stereotype.Controller;
import org.springframework.ui.Model;
import org.springframework.web.bind.annotation.GetMapping;
import org.springframework.web.bind.annotation.ModelAttribute;
import org.springframework.web.bind.annotation.PostMapping;
import org.springframework.web.bind.annotation.RequestMapping;

import com.example.application.service.UserApplicationService;
import com.example.form.SignupForm;

import lombok.extern.slf4j.Slf4j;

@Controller
@RequestMapping("/user")
@Slf4j
public class SignupController {

    @Autowired
    private UserApplicationService userApplicationService;

    /** Display the user signup screen */
    @GetMapping("/signup")
```

```
public String getSignup(Model model, Locale locale,
        @ModelAttribute SignupForm form) {
    // Get gender
    Map<String, Integer> genderMap = userApplicationService.getGenderMap(locale);
    model.addAttribute("genderMap", genderMap);

    // Transition to user signup screen
    return "user/signup";
}

/** User signup process */
@PostMapping("/signup")
public String postSignup(@ModelAttribute SignupForm form) {

    log.info(form.toString());

    // Redirect to login screen
    return "redirect:/login";
}
}
```

Point: @ModelAttribute

If you add this annotation, the instance will be automatically registered in "Model". Explaining with sample code, it is an image that automatically writes the following code.

[@ModelAttribute image]

```
model.addAttribute("signupForm", form);
```

A lowercase string (signupForm) with the beginning of the class name is registered in the "Model" key. You can pass instances to the screen by registering them in the "Model".

Note: @Slf4j

@Slf4j is an annotation of Lombok. If you attach this to the class, you can easily log it using slf4j.

Annotating this class provides a static variable called "log". You can easily output the log by using the method of that variable. In the sample code, it is the following part.

[SignupController.java] (Log output part)

```
log.info(form.toString());
```

The above code outputs info level log. There are other methods for each log output level. For example, you can use the debug method to output debug level logs.

Finally, modify the user signup screen. The part where the background color is changed is the modified part.

[signup.html]

```
<!DOCTYPE html>
<html xmlns:th="http://www.thymeleaf.org">
<head>
  …(Omitted)
</head>
<body class="bg-light">
 <form id="signup-form" method="post" action="/user/signup"
   class="form-signup" th:object="${signupForm}">
  <h1 class="text-center" th:text="#{user.signup.title}"></h1>
  <!-- User ID -->
  <div class="form-group">
   <label for="userId" th:text="#{userId}"></label>
   <input type="text" class="form-control" th:field="*{userId}"/>
  </div>
  <!-- Password -->
  <div class="form-group" >
   <label for="password" th:text="#{password}"></label>
   <input type="text" class="form-control" th:field="*{password}"/>
  </div>
  <!-- User Name -->
  <div class="form-group">
   <label for="userName" th:text="#{userName}"></label>
   <input type="text" class="form-control" th:field="*{userName}"/>
  </div>
  <!-- Birthday -->
  <div class="form-group">
   <label for="birthday" th:text="#{birthday}"></label>
   <input type="text" class="form-control" placeholder="dd/MM/yyyy"
      th:field="*{birthday}"/>
  </div>
  <!-- Age -->
  <div class="form-group">
   <label for="age" th:text="#{age}"></label>
   <input type="text" class="form-control" th:field="*{age}"/>
  </div>
  <!-- Gender -->
  <div class="form-group">
   <div th:each="item : ${genderMap}" class="form-check-inline">
    <input type="radio" class="form-check-input" th:value="${item.value}"
      th:field="*{gender}"/>
    <label class="form-check-label" th:text="${item.key}"></label>
   </div>
  </div>
  <!-- Signup button -->
  <input type="submit" th:value="#{user.signup.btn}"
    class="btn btn-primary w-100 mt-3" />
 </form>
</body>
```

81

```
</html>
```

Points: "th:object" and "th:field"

You can use "th:field" to bind Java classes and screen input. Normally, it is written as follows.

[Use only "th:field"]

```
<input type="text" class="form-control" th:field="${signupForm.userId}"/>
```

Bind with ${Model's registered key name.field name}.

Key name registered in "Model" can be omitted if it is in the tag where "th:object" is written.

[Use "th:object" and "th:field"]

```
<form id="signup-form" method="post" action="/user/signup"
    class="form-signup" th:object="${signupForm}">
...
    <input type="text" class="form-control" th:field="*{userId}"/>
...
</form>
```

You can only bind with "*{field name}".

Note: "th:field"

The HTML input tag does not have an attribute called field. So what kind of HTML does it look like with the "th:field" attribute? If you check the HTML that is actually generated, the result will be as follows.

[Before conversion]

```
<input type="text" class="form-control" th:field="*{userId}"/>
```

[After conversion]

```
<input type="text" class="form-control" id="userId" name="userId"/>
```

The "th:field" attribute converts the field name to the id, name attribute.

Execution

Run Spring Boot and access the following URL.

[URL]
http://localhost:8080/user/signup

[Execution result]

Enter the value on the screen and click the [signup] button. The login screen is displayed, but the following log is output.

[Log] (Excerpt)

SignupForm(userId=tom, password=password, userName=Tom, birthday=Wed Nov 05 00:00:00 JST 1986, age=34, gender=1)

The screen input contents are output to the log. This completes the binding.

6.2.2 Edit error messages

Overview

You can now bind, but there is one problem. If the binding fails, an error screen will be displayed. For example, if a character string is inserted in a place where a date type and a numeric type are input, binding fails.

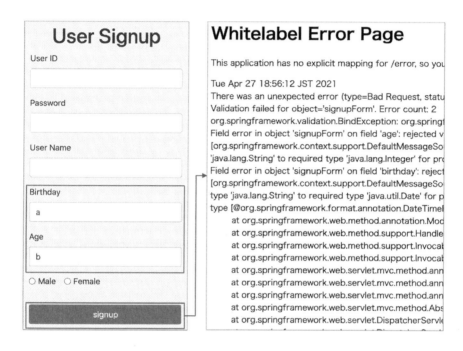

Actually, you should limit the input contents with JavaScript on the screen. However, unexpected values may be sent due to JavaScript bugs or unauthorized access. In case of such a case, fix it so that an error message is displayed when the binding fails.

[User signup screen] (Fixed)

Directory

The directory structure is as follows. The part where the background color is changed is the new part to be added.

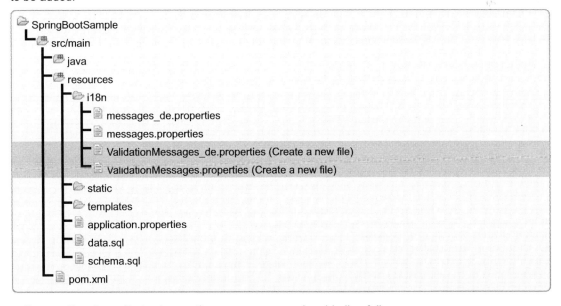

Prepare the above file to change the error message when binding fails.

Source Code

Modify application.properties so that you can get messages from the properties file. The part where the background color is changed is the modified part.

[application.properties]

```
# DataSource
spring.datasource.url=jdbc:h2:mem:testdb;DB_CLOSE_DELAY=-1;DB_CLOSE_ON_EXIT=FALSE
spring.datasource.driver-class-name=org.h2.Driver
spring.datasouce.username=sa
spring.datasouce.password=
spring.datasource.sql-script-encoding=UTF-8
spring.datasource.initialize=true
spring.datasource.schema=classpath:schema.sql
spring.datasource.data=classpath:data.sql

# H2DB
spring.h2.console.enabled=true

# message
spring.messages.basename=i18n/messages,i18n/ValidationMessages
```

Note: ValidationMessages

In spring.messages.basename, you can specify multiple message files separated by commas.

It is up to the application to aggregate all messages into a single file or to split the file. When splitting files, be careful not to duplicate key names.

Next, edit the error message when binding fails.

[ValidationMessages.properties]

```
# =======================
# Bind error message
# =======================
# Pattern1
typeMismatch.signupForm.age=Please enter a number
typeMismatch.signupForm.birthday=Please enter in dd/MM/yyyy format

# Pattern2
#typeMismatch.age=Please enter a number(Pattern2)
#typeMismatch.birthday=Please enter in dd/MM/yyyy format(Pattern2)

# Pattern3
#typeMismatch.int=Please enter a number(Pattern3)
#typeMismatch.java.lang.Integer=Please enter a number(Pattern3)
#typeMismatch.java.util.Date=Please enter in dd/MM/yyyy format(Pattern3)
```

Point: Binding Error Message

There are three ways to set the binding error message:

[How to Configure Binding Error Messages]

Pattern	Setting method	Example
1	typeMismatch.Model key.field name=error message	typeMismatch.signupForm.age=Please enter a number
2	typeMismatch.field=error message	typeMismatch.age=Please enter a number
3	typeMismatch.Data type=error message	typeMismatch.int=Please enter a number

In the sample code, the error message is set by the method of pattern 1. Other patterns are commented out.

In Pattern 1, an error message is set for each Model key and field name. Pattern 2 sets an error message for each field name. "typeMismatch.age" sets the same error message for all "age" fields. Pattern 3 sets an error message for each data type. "typeMismatch.int" sets all int fields to the same error message. For "Integer" types, you must also include "typeMismatch.java.lang.Integer" and the package name.

By the way, if you don't set an error message, the default message will be displayed.

If you have a German language file, you can make it multilingual.
[ValidationMessages_de.properties]

```
# ========================
# Bind error message
# ========================
# Pattern1
typeMismatch.signupForm.age=Bitte gebe eine Nummer ein
typeMismatch.signupForm.birthday=Bitte geben Sie im Format TT/MM/JJJJ ein

# Pattern2
#typeMismatch.age=Bitte gebe eine Nummer ein(Pattern2)
#typeMismatch.birthday=Bitte geben Sie im Format TT/MM/JJJJ ein(Pattern2)

# Pattern3
#typeMismatch.int=Bitte gebe eine Nummer ein(Pattern3)
#typeMismatch.java.lang.Integer=Bitte gebe eine Nummer ein(Pattern3)
#typeMismatch.java.util.Date=Bitte geben Sie im Format TT/MM/JJJJ ein(Pattern3)
```

Modify the controller so that it returns to the user signup screen when an error occurs in the input content of the screen. The part where the background color is changed is the modified part.

[SignupController.java]

```java
package com.example.controller;

import java.util.Locale;
import java.util.Map;

import org.springframework.beans.factory.annotation.Autowired;
import org.springframework.stereotype.Controller;
import org.springframework.ui.Model;
import org.springframework.validation.BindingResult;
import org.springframework.web.bind.annotation.GetMapping;
import org.springframework.web.bind.annotation.ModelAttribute;
import org.springframework.web.bind.annotation.PostMapping;
import org.springframework.web.bind.annotation.RequestMapping;

import com.example.application.service.UserApplicationService;
import com.example.form.SignupForm;

import lombok.extern.slf4j.Slf4j;

@Controller
@RequestMapping("/user")
@Slf4j
public class SignupController {

    @Autowired
    private UserApplicationService userApplicationService;

    /** Display the user signup screen */
    @GetMapping("/signup")
    public String getSignup(Model model, Locale locale,
            @ModelAttribute SignupForm form) {
        …(Omitted)
    }

    /** User signup process */
    @PostMapping("/signup")
    public String postSignup(Model model, Locale locale,
            @ModelAttribute SignupForm form,
            BindingResult bindingResult) {

        // Input check result
        if (bindingResult.hasErrors()) {
            // NG: Return to the user signup screen
            return getSignup(model, locale, form);
        }

        log.info(form.toString());
```

```
    // Redirect to login screen
    return "redirect:/login";
  }
}
```

Point: BindingResult

Whether bind error and validation error has occurred, it can be found in the method of BindingResult class. If the result of the hasErrors() method is true, then you have a bind or validation error.

Finally, modify the user signup screen to display error messages. The part where the background color is changed is the modified part.

[signup.html]

```html
<!DOCTYPE html>
<html xmlns:th="http://www.thymeleaf.org">
<head>
  ...(Omitted)
</head>
<body class="bg-light">
  <form id="signup-form" method="post" action="/user/signup"
    class="form-signup" th:object="${signupForm}">
    <h1 class="text-center" th:text="#{user.signup.title}"></h1>
    <!-- User ID -->
    <div class="form-group">
      <label for="userId" th:text="#{userId}"></label>
      <input type="text" class="form-control" th:field="*{userId}"
        th:errorclass="is-invalid"/>
      <div class="invalid-feedback" th:errors="*{userId}"></div>
    </div>
    <!-- Password -->
    <div class="form-group" >
      <label for="password" th:text="#{password}"></label>
      <input type="text" class="form-control" th:field="*{password}"
        th:errorclass="is-invalid"/>
      <div class="invalid-feedback" th:errors="*{password}"></div>
    </div>
    <!-- User Name -->
    <div class="form-group">
      <label for="userName" th:text="#{userName}"></label>
      <input type="text" class="form-control" th:field="*{userName}"
        th:errorclass="is-invalid"/>
      <div class="invalid-feedback" th:errors="*{userName}"></div>
    </div>
    <!-- Birthday -->
    <div class="form-group">
      <label for="birthday" th:text="#{birthday}"></label>
```

```html
      <input type="text" class="form-control" placeholder="dd/MM/yyyy"
        th:field="*{birthday}" th:errorclass="is-invalid"/>
      <div class="invalid-feedback" th:errors="*{birthday}"></div>
    </div>
    <!-- Age -->
    <div class="form-group">
      <label for="age" th:text="#{age}"></label>
      <input type="text" class="form-control" th:field="*{age}"
        th:errorclass="is-invalid"/>
      <div class="invalid-feedback" th:errors="*{age}"></div>
    </div>
    <!-- Gender -->
    <div class="form-group">
      <div th:each="item : ${genderMap}" class="form-check-inline">
        <input type="radio" class="form-check-input" th:value="${item.value}"
          th:field="*{gender}" th:errorclass="is-invalid"/>
        <label class="form-check-label" th:text="${item.key}"></label>
      </div>
      <div class="text-danger" th:if="${#fields.hasErrors('gender')}"
        th:errors="*{gender}">
      </div>
    </div>
    <!-- Signup button -->
    <input type="submit" th:value="#{user.signup.btn}"
      class="btn btn-primary w-100 mt-3" />
  </form>
</body>
</html>
```

Point 1: "th:errorclass"

"th:errorclass" is valid when used in the same tag as "th:field". If an error occurs in the field specified by "th:field", "th:errorclass" will add the CSS class. In the sample code, a CSS class called "is-invalid" provided by Bootstrap is added.

[signup.html]

```html
<input type="text" class="form-control" th:field="*{userId}"
  th:errorclass="is-invalid"/>
```

If userId encounters an error, the "is-invalid" class is added.

Point 2: "th:errors"

Specify the field name in "th: errors". If there was an error in the specified field, an error message will be displayed in the tag.

[signup.html]

```
<div class="form-group">
  <label for="userId" th:text="#{userId}"></label>
  <input type="text" class="form-control" th:field="*{userId}"
    th:errorclass="is-invalid"/>
  <div class="invalid-feedback" th:errors="*{userId}"></div>
</div>
```

In the sample code, the "invalid-feedback" CSS class provided by Bootstrap is set. This means that if there is no tag with the "is-invalid" class in the same tag, the tag will not be displayed.

Point 3: "th:if"

With: "th:if" attribute, you can decide whether to generate a tag depending on the conditions. If the conditions are met, a tag will be generated.

You can check if an error has occurred in a field by writing ${#fields.hasErrors('field name')} in the condition of "th:if".

[signup.html]

```
<div class="text-danger" th:if="${#fields.hasErrors('gender')}"
    th:errors="*{gender}">
</div>
```

Execution

Run Spring Boot and access the following URL.

[URL]

http://localhost:8080/user/signup

Enter characters for the birthday and age and click the "signup" button.

[Execution result]

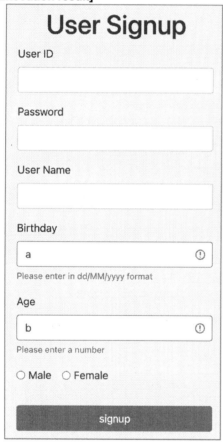

If you see an error message, you're done.

6.3 Validation

From here on, you will create a validation (input check).

- Implementation of validation
- Edit error messages
- Setting the validation execution order

6.3.1 Implementation of validation

Overview

Validation is an input check. Spring makes it easy to implement validation by simply annotating it.

[User signup screen] (After Validation Implementation)

Directory

There is no change in the directory structure.

Source Code

A library is required to use validation. Therefore, add the following code in the dependencies tag of pom.xml. The part where the background color is changed is the added part.

[pom.xml]

```
<dependencies>
...
<!-- validator -->
<dependency>
  <groupId>org.springframework.boot</groupId>
  <artifactId>spring-boot-starter-validation</artifactId>
</dependency>
...
</dependencies>
```

Modify the form class that receives input from the screen. The part where the background color is changed is the modified part.

[SignupForm.java]

```java
package com.example.form;

import java.util.Date;

import javax.validation.constraints.Email;
import javax.validation.constraints.Max;
import javax.validation.constraints.Min;
import javax.validation.constraints.NotBlank;
import javax.validation.constraints.NotNull;
import javax.validation.constraints.Pattern;

import org.hibernate.validator.constraints.Length;
import org.springframework.format.annotation.DateTimeFormat;

import lombok.Data;

@Data
public class SignupForm {

    @NotBlank
    @Email
    private String userId;
```

```
@NotBlank
@Length(min = 4, max = 100)
@Pattern(regexp = "^[a-zA-Z0-9]+$")
private String password;

@NotBlank
private String userName;

@DateTimeFormat(pattern = "dd/MM/yyyy")
@NotNull
private Date birthday;

@Min(20)
@Max(100)
private Integer age;

@NotNull
private Integer gender;
}
```

Point: Validation Annotation

The following annotations are provided to implement validation:

[Annotation List]

Class	Annotation	Description	Example
Bean Validation	@NotNull	Check that it is not null.	@NotNull String userName;
	@NotEmpty	Check that the string or collection is null or not empty.	@NotEmpty LIst<User> userList;
	@NotBlank	Checks that the string is not only null, blank, or blank spaces.	@NotBlank String password;
	@Max	Checks whether the value is less than or equal to the specified value.	@Max(100) int age;
	@Min	Checks whether the value is greater than or equal to the specified value.	@Min(20) int age;
	@Size	Checks if the length of the string and the size of the Collection are within the specified	@Size(min = 0, max = 20) List<User> userList;

Class	Annotation	Description	Example
		range.	
	@AssertTrue	Check if it is true.	@AssertTrue boolean marriage;
	@AssertFalse	Check for false.	@AssertFalse boolean marriage;
	@Pattern	Checks for a match with the specified regular expression.	@Pattern() String password;
	@Email	Checks whether the string is in email address format.	@Email String userId;
Hibernate Validator	@Range	Checks whether a numeric value is within a specified range.	@Range(min = 20, max = 100) int age;
	@Length	Checks if the length of the string is within the specified range.	@Length(min = 8, max = 100) String password;
	@CreditCardNumber	Checks whether the string is in credit card number format.	@CreditCardNumber String cardNumber;
	@URL	Checks whether a string is in URL format.	@URL String url;

There are other validation annotations available. For details, please refer to the official Hibernate Validator page.

By the way, Not Null, Not Empty and Not Blank have the following differences.

[Difference between NotNull and NotEmpty and NotBlank]

Annotations	null	Empty character	Blank
@NotNull	NG	OK	OK
@NotEmpty	NG	NG	OK
@NotBlank	NG	NG	NG

NG: The validation result will be an error.

Finally, modify the user-signup controller to perform validation. The part where the background color is changed is the modified part.

[SignupController.java]

```java
package com.example.controller;

import java.util.Locale;
import java.util.Map;

import org.springframework.beans.factory.annotation.Autowired;
import org.springframework.stereotype.Controller;
import org.springframework.ui.Model;
import org.springframework.validation.BindingResult;
import org.springframework.validation.annotation.Validated;
import org.springframework.web.bind.annotation.GetMapping;
import org.springframework.web.bind.annotation.ModelAttribute;
import org.springframework.web.bind.annotation.PostMapping;
import org.springframework.web.bind.annotation.RequestMapping;

import com.example.application.service.UserApplicationService;
import com.example.form.SignupForm;

import lombok.extern.slf4j.Slf4j;

@Controller
@RequestMapping("/user")
@Slf4j
public class SignupController {

    @Autowired
    private UserApplicationService userApplicationService;

    /** Display the user signup screen */
    @GetMapping("/signup")
```

```
@GetMapping("/signup")
public String getSignup(Model model, Locale locale,
    @ModelAttribute SignupForm form) {
  …(Omitted)
}

/** User signup process */
@PostMapping("/signup")
public String postSignup(Model model, Locale locale,
    @ModelAttribute @Validated SignupForm form,
    BindingResult bindingResult) {

  // Input check result
  if (bindingResult.hasErrors()) {
    // NG: Return to the user signup screen
    return getSignup(model, locale, form);
  }

  log.info(form.toString());

  // Redirect to login screen
  return "redirect:/login";
  }
}
```

Point: @Validated

If you add the @Validated annotation, validation will be performed.

Execution

Run Spring Boot and access the following URL.

[URL]
http://localhost:8080/user/signup

Please click "signup" without entering anything on the screen.

[Execution result]

If an error message appears, the validation is complete.

Note: Validation Results

The result of validation is put in "BindingResult". The processing when a validation error occurs can be implemented by performing the same processing as the binding error. The error message is displayed in the same way as for a bind error. These processes are implemented in [6.2.2 Editing error messages]. Therefore, the sample code in this book will display an error message.

6.3.2 Edit Error Messages

Overview

Edit the validation error message. You can edit the error message simply by modifying ValidationMessages.properties.

[User signup screen] (After editing error messages)

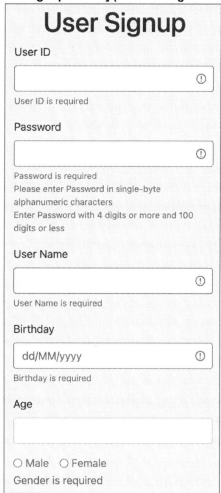

Directory

There is no change in the directory structure.

Source Code

Add validation error messages to the properties file. The part where the background color is changed is the modified part.

[ValidationMessages.properties]

```
# =======================
# Bind error message
# =======================
# Pattern1
typeMismatch.signupForm.age=Please enter a number
typeMismatch.signupForm.birthday=Please enter in dd/MM/yyyy format

# Pattern2
#typeMismatch.age=Please enter a number(Pattern2)
#typeMismatch.birthday=Please enter in dd/MM/yyyy format(Pattern2)

# Pattern3
#typeMismatch.int=Please enter a number(Pattern3)
#typeMismatch.java.lang.Integer=Please enter a number(Pattern3)
#typeMismatch.java.util.Date=Please enter in dd/MM/yyyy format(Pattern3)

# =======================
# Validation error message
# =======================
NotBlank={0} is required
Email=Please enter {0} in email address format
Length=Enter {0} with {2} digits or more and {1} digits or less
Pattern=Please enter {0} in single-byte alphanumeric characters
NotNull={0} is required
Min=Enter {1} or more for {0}
Max=For {0}, enter {1} or less
```

Point: Validation Error Message

There are several ways to edit validation error messages. Of these, it is easiest to configure [Annotation name = error message].

Characters such as {0} and {1} are included in the sample code. This is a parameter in the message. You can use parameters to display variable messages. For example, {0} is the field name.

Example: When the input result is an error with @NotNull

Setting value	Display result
NotNull={0} is required	Gender is required

The value of the attribute set in the annotation is displayed for the numbers after {0}.

Example: @Length(min = 4, max = 100)

- {1} = 100(value of max)
- {2} = 4(value of min)

Which numbers contain which attribute values is set in ascending order by attribute name. Since the order of max is earlier than min, it is set as above.

For multilingual support, also edit the properties file for German. The part where the background color is changed is the modified part.

[ValidationMessages_de.properties]

```
# ========================
# Bind error message
# ========================
# Pattern1
typeMismatch.signupForm.age=Bitte gebe eine Nummer ein
typeMismatch.signupForm.birthday=Bitte geben Sie im Format TT/MM/JJJJ ein

# Pattern2
#typeMismatch.age=Bitte gebe eine Nummer ein(Pattern2)
#typeMismatch.birthday=Bitte geben Sie im Format TT/MM/JJJJ ein(Pattern2)

# Pattern3
#typeMismatch.int=Bitte gebe eine Nummer ein(Pattern3)
#typeMismatch.java.lang.Integer=Bitte gebe eine Nummer ein(Pattern3)
#typeMismatch.java.util.Date=Bitte geben Sie im Format TT/MM/JJJJ ein(Pattern3)

# ========================
# Validation error message
# ========================
NotBlank={0} ist erforderlich is required
Email=Bitte geben Sie {0} im E-Mail-Adressformat ein
Length=Geben Sie {0} mit {2} Ziffern oder mehr und {1} Ziffern oder weniger ein
Pattern=Bitte geben Sie {0} in alphanumerischen Einzelbyte-Zeichen ein
NotNull={0} ist erforderlich is required
Min=Geben Sie {1} oder mehr für {0} ein
Max=Geben Sie für {0} {1} oder weniger ein
```

I explained that {0} in the error message contains the field name. However, if nothing is set, the field name of the form class will be displayed as it is.

Example: Nothing is set in the field name

Setting value	Display result
NotNull={0} is required	gender is required

Next, edit messages.properties to change the display of the field name. The way to edit is to set "field name = character". Only the gender field name is not set. Other field names have already been set. The part where the background color is changed is the modified part.

[messages.properties]

```
user.signup.title=User Signup
user.signup.btn=signup
userId=User ID
password=Password
userName=User Name
birthday=Birthday
age=Age
male=Male
female=Female
gender=Gender
```

For multilingual support, we will also modify the message file for German. The part where the background color is changed is the modified part.

[messages_de.properties]

```
user.signup.title=Anmeldung
user.signup.btn=anmeldung
userId=Benutzer-ID
password=Passwort
userName=Benutzername
birthday=Geburtstag
age=Alter
male=Männlich
female=Weiblich
gender=Geschlecht
```

Execution

Run Spring Boot and access the following URL.

[URL]

http://localhost:8080/user/signup

Enter the values on the screen so that a validation error occurs and click the signup button.

[Execution result]

If the error message changes, you're done.

Note: How to Edit Validation Error Messages

There are other ways to edit validation error messages.

[How to Configure Validation Error Messages]

Pattern	Setting method	Setting example
1	Annotation name.ModelAttribute key name.Field name=error message	NotBlank.signupForm.userId=Please enter user ID
2	Annotation name.Field name=error message	NotBlank.userId=Please enter user ID
3	Annotation name.Field data type=error message	NotBlank.java.lang.String=Required input
4	Unique key name=error message	require_check=Required input

Patterns 1 to 3 can be set by editing only the property file. Pattern 4 must map the key names of the annotations and messages. Set as follows.

Example: Pattern 4 setting
[ValidationMessages.properties]

```
require_check=Required input
```

[SignupForm.java]

```java
public class SignupForm {

    @NotBlank(message = "{require_check}")
    @Email
    private String userId;
    ...
```

6.3.3 Setting the validation execution order

Overview

If the validation result is NG, all error messages will be displayed. Whether or not to allow it depends on the design. If you want to set the validation execution order, set the validation group.

[Validation Group Settings]

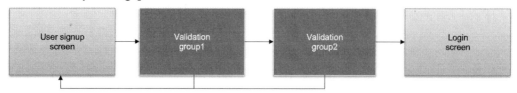

If Validation Group 1 is OK, proceed with Group 2. If the check result is NG for each group, the screen returns to the user signup screen.

On the User signup screen, modify the validation to occur in the following order:

1. Required input check
2. Input content check

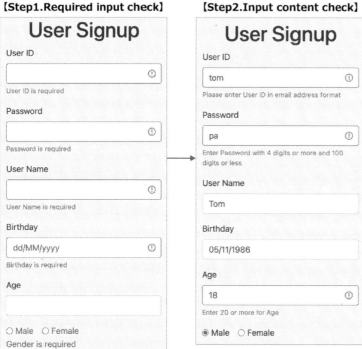

Directory

The directory structure is as follows. The part where the background color is changed is the new part to be added.

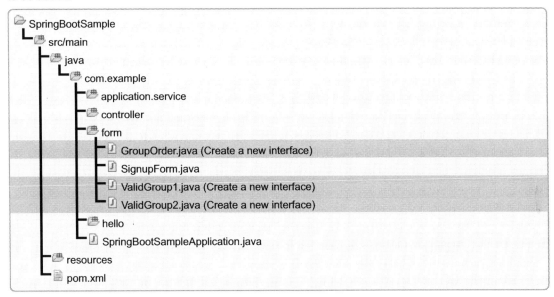

※Create an interface, not a Java class.

Source Code

ValidGroup1 and ValidGroup2 are empty interfaces.
[ValidGroup1.java]

```
package com.example.form;

public interface ValidGroup1 {

}
```

[ValidGroup2.java]

```
package com.example.form;

public interface ValidGroup2 {

}
```

Set the order of validation in GroupOrder.

[GroupOrder.java]

```java
package com.example.form;

import javax.validation.GroupSequence;

@GroupSequence({ ValidGroup1.class, ValidGroup2.class })
public interface GroupOrder {

}
```

Point: @GroupSequence

The @GroupSequence annotation sets the order of validation. Validation is performed in the order of the interfaces set from the left.

In the sample code, it is checked in the following order:

1. ValidGroup1
2. ValidGroup2

Then you associate the order of validation with the validation for the form class. The part where the background color is changed is the modified part.

[SignupForm.java]

```java
@Data
public class SignupForm {

    @NotBlank(groups = ValidGroup1.class)
    @Email(groups = ValidGroup2.class)
    private String userId;

    @NotBlank(groups = ValidGroup1.class)
    @Length(min = 4, max = 100, groups = ValidGroup2.class)
    @Pattern(regexp = "^[a-zA-Z0-9]+$", groups = ValidGroup2.class)
    private String password;

    @NotBlank(groups = ValidGroup1.class)
    private String userName;

    @DateTimeFormat(pattern = "dd/MM/yyyy")
    @NotNull(groups = ValidGroup1.class)
    private Date birthday;

    @Min(value = 20, groups = ValidGroup2.class)
    @Max(value = 100, groups = ValidGroup2.class)
    private Integer age;
```

```
    @NotNull(groups = ValidGroup1.class)
    private Integer gender;
}
```

To map the order of validation, specify the interface in the groups attribute of each annotation.

Finally, modify the Signup Controller.The part where the background color is changed is the modified part.

[SignupController.java]

```
@Controller
@RequestMapping("/user")
@Slf4j
public class SignupController {

    @Autowired
    private UserApplicationService userApplicationService;

    /** Display the user signup screen */
    @GetMapping("/signup")
    public String getSignup(Model model, Locale locale,
            @ModelAttribute SignupForm form) {
        ...(Omitted)
    }

    /** User signup process */
    @PostMapping("/signup")
    public String postSignup(Model model, Locale locale,
            @ModelAttribute @Validated(GroupOrder.class) SignupForm form,
            BindingResult bindingResult) {

        // Input check result
        if (bindingResult.hasErrors()) {
            // NG: Return to the user signup screen
            return getSignup(model, locale, form);
        }

        log.info(form.toString());

        // Redirect to login screen
        return "redirect:/login";
    }
}
```

You can specify GroupOrder.class in the @Validated annotation to reflect the validation order setting.

Execution

Run Spring Boot and access the following URL.

[URL]
http://localhost:8080/user/signup

First, click "signup" without entering any value on the screen. Then enter the value on the screen and click "signup".

【Step1.Required input check】   ### 【Step2.Input content check】

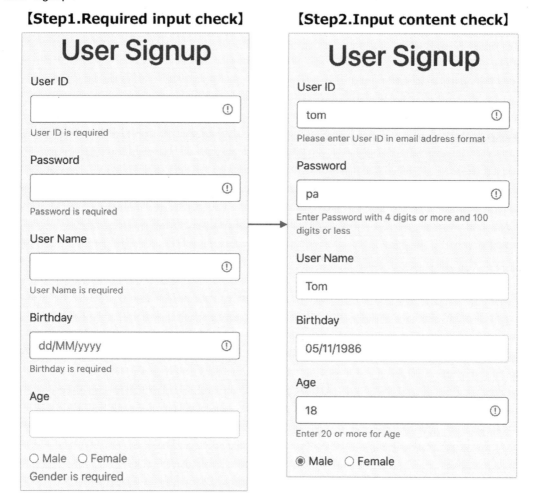

If the order of validation is set, it is complete.

Summary

Here's what you've learned in this chapter.

[Create Screen]

- "webjars" makes it easy to use the library.
- You can use "messages.properties" to manage messages.
- You can use "messages.properties" to support multiple languages.

[Binding]

- The Java class to be bound is registered in "Model".
- The screen uses "th:field" to map Java class fields.

[Validation]

- Annotations can be used to implement validation.
- Use "BindingResult" to determine if a validation error occurred.
- The @GroupSequence annotation allows you to set the order of validation.

[Other]

- Use "BindingResult" to determine if an error occurred during binding or validation.
- You can get error messages with "th:errors" attribute.
- You can add a CSS class on error with the "th:errorclass" attribute.
- Error messages can be edited in the properties file.

7. Screen Layout

In this chapter, you will learn how to create screen layouts.

7.1 Implementing the Screen Layout

Overview

It is common to use the layout function for screen creation. With the layout, because the need to write a common HTML on each screen is eliminated. You can also make it easier to change the layout by preparing a different layout file.

The examples in this book create the following layout screens:

[Layout configuration]

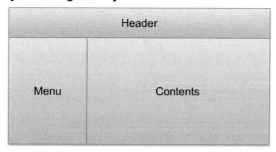

Specifically, create the following user list screen.

[user list screen]

When you log in, create an application that transitions to the user list screen.

To make this screen, we will make the following four HTML files.

- Layout
- Header
- Menu
- Content

Directory

The directory structure is as follows. The part where the background color is changed is the new part to be added.

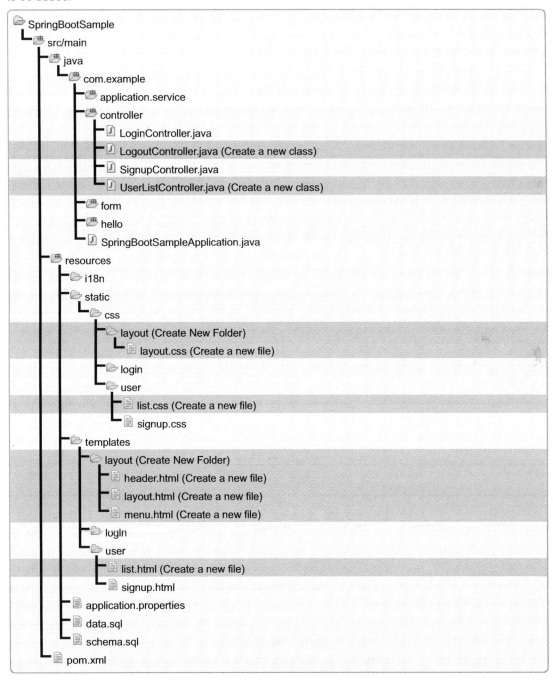

```
SpringBootSample
  src/main
    java
      com.example
        application.service
        controller
            LoginController.java
            LogoutController.java (Create a new class)
            SignupController.java
            UserListController.java (Create a new class)
        form
        hello
        SpringBootSampleApplication.java
    resources
      i18n
      static
        css
          layout (Create New Folder)
              layout.css (Create a new file)
          login
          user
              list.css (Create a new file)
              signup.css
      templates
        layout (Create New Folder)
            header.html (Create a new file)
            layout.html (Create a new file)
            menu.html (Create a new file)
        login
        user
            list.html (Create a new file)
            signup.html
      application.properties
      data.sql
      schema.sql
  pom.xml
```

Source code

First, add a library for creating layouts in Thymeleaf. Add the following code in the dependencies tag of pom.xml. The part where the background color is changed is the added part.

[pom.xml]

```
<dependencies>
  ...
  <!-- thymeleaf-layout-dialect -->
  <dependency>
    <groupId>nz.net.ultraq.thymeleaf</groupId>
    <artifactId>thymeleaf-layout-dialect</artifactId>
  </dependency>
  ...
</dependencies>
```

Create a controller for the user list screen.

[UserListController.java]

```
package com.example.controller;

import org.springframework.stereotype.Controller;
import org.springframework.web.bind.annotation.GetMapping;
import org.springframework.web.bind.annotation.RequestMapping;

@Controller
@RequestMapping("/user")
public class UserListController {

    /** Display user list screen */
    @GetMapping("/list")
    public String getUserList() {
        // Display user list screen
        return "user/list";
    }
}
```

Modify the controller of the login screen so that you can transition to the user list screen. The part where the background color is changed is the modified part.

[LoginController.java.java]

```
package com.example.controller;

import org.springframework.stereotype.Controller;
import org.springframework.web.bind.annotation.GetMapping;
import org.springframework.web.bind.annotation.PostMapping;

@Controller
```

```
public class LoginController {

  /** Display login screen */
  @GetMapping("/login")
  public String getLogin() {
    return "login/login";
  }

  /** Redirect to user list screen */
  @PostMapping("/login")
  public String postLogin() {
    return "redirect:/user/list";
  }
}
```

Create a controller for logout.
[LogoutController.java]

```
package com.example.controller;

import org.springframework.stereotype.Controller;
import org.springframework.web.bind.annotation.PostMapping;

@Controller
@Slf4j
public class LogoutController {

  /** Redirect to login screen */
  @PostMapping("/logout")
  public String postLogout() {
    log.info("Logout");
    return "redirect:/login";
  }
}
```

Create HTML for the screen layout.
[layout.html]

```
<!DOCTYPE html>
<html xmlns:th="http://www.thymeleaf.org"
  xmlns:layout="http://www.ultraq.net.nz/thymeleaf/layout">
<head>
<meta charset="UTF-8"></meta>
<meta name="viewport" content="width=device-width, initial-scale=1, shrink-to-fit=no">
<!-- Read Common CSS -->
<link rel="stylesheet" th:href="@{/webjars/bootstrap/css/bootstrap.min.css}">
<link rel="stylesheet" th:href="@{/css/layout/layout.css}">
<!-- Read Common JS -->
<script th:src="@{/webjars/jquery/jquery.min.js}" defer></script>
```

```
  <script th:src="@{/webjars/bootstrap/js/bootstrap.min.js}" defer></script>
  <title></title>
</head>
<body>
  <!-- Header -->
  <nav layout:replace="~{layout/header::header}"></nav>
  <!-- Menu -->
  <div class="container-fluid">
    <div class="row">
      <nav class="col-sm-2 bg-light sidebar pt-2">
        <div layout:replace="~{layout/menu::menu}"></div>
      </nav>
    </div>
  </div>
  <!-- Content -->
  <div class="container-fluid">
    <div class="row">
      <div class="col-sm-10 offset-sm-2 main">
        <div layout:fragment="content"></div>
      </div>
    </div>
  </div>
</body>
</html>
```

Point 1: "xmlns:layout"

To use layouts with Thymeleaf, add the [xmlns:layout="http://www.ultraq.net.nz/thymeleaf/layout"] to the html tags.

Point 2: "layout:replace"

To read other HTML files, use the "layout:replace" attribute. Specify the value in the following format:

[Format of layout:replace]

```
~{file-path::key-name}
```

For the file path, specify a relative path from "src/main/resources/templates". Specify any value for the key name. Explaining with the sample code, the other HTML file is read in the following part.

[layout.html]

```
<!-- header -->
<nav layout:replace="~{layout/header::header}"></nav>
```

In this case, the "src/main/resources/templates/layout/header.html" file is the target. Then, read the part with the key name header in that file.

Point 3: "layout:fragment"

To read other HTML files, use the "layout:fragment" attribute. The value of this attribute can be any key name.

"layout:replace" and "layout: fragment" both read other HTML files. The difference between "layout:replace" and "layout:fragment" will be explained later.

[header.html]

```
<!DOCTYPE html>
<html xmlns:th="http://www.thymeleaf.org"
  xmlns:layout="http://www.ultraq.net.nz/thymeleaf/layout"
  layout:decorate="~{layout/layout}">
<head>
</head>
<body>
 <nav layout:fragment="header"
    class="navbar navbar-inverse navbar-fixed-top navbar-dark bg-dark">
   <div class="container-fluid">
   <div class="navbar-header">
    <a class="navbar-brand" href="#">SpringSample</a>
   </div>
   <form method="post" th:action="@{/logout}">
    <button class="btn btn-link pull-right navbar-brand" type="submit">
     Logout
    </button>
   </form>
  </div>
 </nav>
</body>
</html>
```

Point 1: "layout:decorate"

Specifies which layout to include this HTML in. Enter in the following format:

[Format of layout:decorate]

```
~{file path}
```

For the file path, specify a relative path from "src/main/resources/templates". In the sample code, "src/main/resources/templates/layout/layout.html" is specified.

Point 2: "layout:fragment"

Specifies a key name that is referenced by the layout's HTML. As described in the sample code in this book, the following points must match:

[layout.html]

```
<nav layout:replace="~{layout/header::header}"></nav>
```

[header.html]

```
<nav layout:fragment="header"
    class="navbar navbar-inverse navbar-fixed-top navbar-dark bg-dark">
```

The header HTML is now embedded in the layout HTML.

Similarly, create HTML for the menu.

[menu.html]

```
<!DOCTYPE html>
<html xmlns:th="http://www.thymeleaf.org"
 xmlns:layout="http://www.ultraq.net.nz/thymeleaf/layout"
 layout:decorate="~{layout/layout}">
<head>
</head>
<body>
  <div layout:fragment="menu" class="bg-light">
   <ul class="nav nav-pills nav-stacked flex-column">
    <li role="presentation">
     <a class="nav-link" th:href="@{'/user/list'}">User list</a>
    </li>
   </ul>
  </div>
</body>
</html>
```

In the same way, create HTML for the user list screen.

[list.html]

```
<!DOCTYPE html>
<html xmlns:th="http://www.thymeleaf.org"
 xmlns:layout="http://www.ultraq.net.nz/thymeleaf/layout"
 layout:decorate="~{layout/layout}">
<head>
 <title>User List</title>
 <!-- Read Dedicated CSS -->
 <link rel="stylesheet" th:href="@{/css/user/list.css}">
</head>
<body>
  <div layout:fragment="content">
   <div class="header border-bottom">
    <h1 class="h2">User List</h1>
```

```
    </div>
  </div>
 </body>
</html>
```

Now create a CSS.

[layout.css]

```
.sidebar {
 position: fixed;
 display: block;
 top: 58px;
 bottom: 0;
 left: 0;
}

.main {
 position: fixed;
 display: block;
 top: 58px;
 bottom: 0;
 padding-left: 20px;
 overflow-y: auto;
 height: calc(100vh - 58px);
}
```

[list.css]

```
.header {
 padding-top: 1rem!important;
 padding-bottom: .5rem!important;
 margin-bottom: 1rem!important;
}

.th-width {
 width: 200px;
}
```

Execution

Run SpringBoot and access the login screen. Please press the "Login" button without entering anything on the screen. The screen will change to the user list screen.

This completes the screen creation using the layout.

Note: Differences Between "layout:replace" and "layout:fragment"

There are slight differences between "layout:replace" and "layout:fragment" in the generated HTML. The differences are as follows:

- "layout:replace" replaces the entire tag.
- "layout:fragment" adds HTML inside the tag.

Specifically, it is as follows.

Sample "layout:replace"

[HTML sample on layout side]

```
<div layout:replace="~{sample/contents::contents}"></div>
```

[HTML sample on content side]

```
<div layout:fragment="contents">
 <p>Sample</p>
</div>
```

[HTML generated by "layout:replace"]

```
<div>
 <p>Sample</p>
</div>
```

In other words, the content-side HTML replaces the layout-side HTML. No layout-side HTML remains.

Sample "layout:fragment"

[HTML sample on layout side]

```
<div layout:fragment="~{contents}" id="sample"></div>
```

[HTML sample on content side]

```
<div layout:fragment="contents">
  <p>Sample</p>
</div>
```

[HTML generated by "layout:fragment"]

```
<div id="sample">
  <div>
    <p>Sample</p>
  </div>
</div>
```

This means that the content-side HTML is added inside the layout-side HTML element.

Note: How to Implement the Screen Layout

Even if you don't add libraries for screen layouts, you can create screen layouts with only the default Thymeleaf functionality. How to do this is to use the attributes "th:replace" and "th:fragment". Both attributes are used the same way as "layout:replace" and "layout:fragment". However, the generated HTML is different depending on whether or not you use a library for screen layouts. Specifically, the elements in the head tag change.

When using "th:replace" and "th:fragment"

[HTML sample on layout side]

```
<head>
  <link rel="stylesheet" th:href="@{/css/common.css}">
  <script th:src="@{/js/common.js}" defer></script>
</head>
```

[HTML sample on content side]

```
<head>
  <title>Sample Content</title>
```

```
  <link rel="stylesheet" th:href="@{/css/sample.css}">
  <script th:src="@{/js/sample.js}" defer></script>
</head>
```

[Generated HTML]

```
<head>
  <link rel="stylesheet" th:href="@{/css/common.css}">
  <script th:src="@{/js/common.js}" defer></script>
</head>
```

In other words, in the "th:replace" attribute, only the head tag on the layout side remains.

When using "layout:replace" and "layout:fragment"

[HTML sample on layout side]

```
<head>
  <link rel="stylesheet" th:href="@{/css/common.css}">
  <script th:src="@{/js/common.js}" defer></script>
</head>
```

[HTML sample on content side]

```
<head>
  <title>Sample Content</title>
  <link rel="stylesheet" th:href="@{/css/sample.css}">
  <script th:src="@{/js/sample.js}" defer></script>
</head>
```

[Generated HTML]

```
<head>
  <title>Sample Content</title>
  <link rel="stylesheet" th:href="@{/css/common.css}">
  <script th:src="@{/js/common.js}" defer></script>
  <link rel="stylesheet" th:href="@{/css/sample.css}">
  <script th:src="@{/js/sample.js}" defer></script>
</head>
```

The "layout:replace" attribute adds the elements inside the content-side head tag inside the layout-side head tag. Therefore, using the layout library makes it easier to create screen layouts.

Summary

Here's what you've learned in this chapter.

[How to create a screen layout]

- Use libraries for screen layouts.
- Add the [xmlns:layout="http://www.ultraq.net.nz/thymeleaf/layout"] in the html tags.

[Layout side HTML]

The layout-side HTML uses the following attributes:

- layout:replace
- layout:fragment

[Content side HTML]

The content-side HTML uses the following attributes:

- layout:fragment

8. MyBatis

In this chapter you will learn about MyBatis for working with databases.

- Overview of MyBatis
- MyBatis basic
- MyBatis advanced
- Transaction

8.1 Overview of MyBatis

MyBatis is an O/R mapper with advanced functions. An O/R mapper is a framework that maps Java classes (objects) and databases. It is called an O/R mapper because it maps Objects to Relations.

In particular, MyBatis maps Object and SQL by an xml file.

Note: SQL

In MyBatis, you can write SQL in java file, but you rarely use it.

8.2 MyBatis basic

First of all, you will learn the basic usage of MyBatis.

- insert
- select...multiple records
- select...1 record
- update/delete

8.2.1 insert

Overview

You can actually register a user on the user signup screen. The data is registered in the H2 database.

[Execution result]

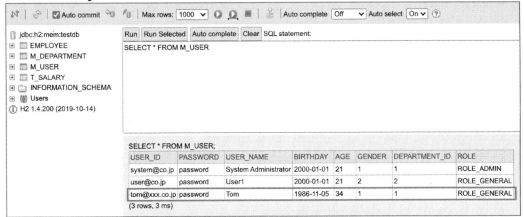

In addition, the initial data for use in the learning after this is also registered.

Directory

The directory structure is as follows. The part where the background color is changed is the new part to be added.

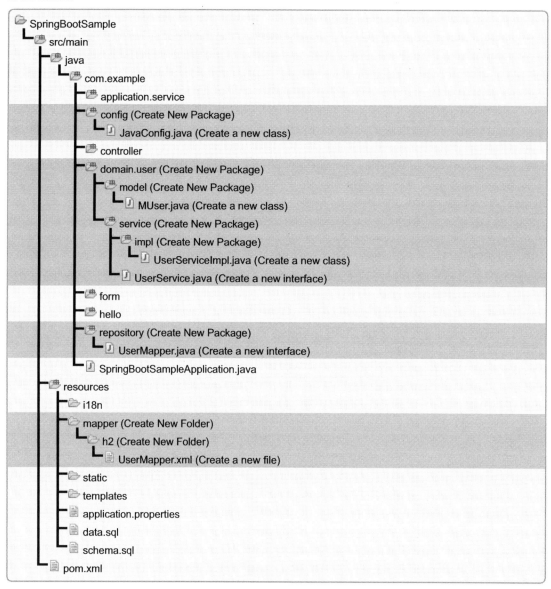

```
SpringBootSample
  src/main
    java
      com.example
        application.service
        config (Create New Package)
          JavaConfig.java (Create a new class)
        controller
        domain.user (Create New Package)
          model (Create New Package)
            MUser.java (Create a new class)
          service (Create New Package)
            impl (Create New Package)
              UserServiceImpl.java (Create a new class)
            UserService.java (Create a new interface)
        form
        hello
        repository (Create New Package)
          UserMapper.java (Create a new interface)
        SpringBootSampleApplication.java
    resources
      i18n
      mapper (Create New Folder)
        h2 (Create New Folder)
          UserMapper.xml (Create a new file)
      static
      templates
      application.properties
      data.sql
      schema.sql
  pom.xml
```

Source Code

First, to download the MyBatis library, add the following code to pom.xml. In addition to MyBatis, you add a useful library called ModelMapper. ModelMapper is a library that copies the contents of an instance. The part where the background color is changed is the added part.

[pom.xml]

```xml
<dependencies>
  ...
  <!-- MyBatis -->
  <dependency>
    <groupId>org.mybatis.spring.boot</groupId>
    <artifactId>mybatis-spring-boot-starter</artifactId>
    <version>2.1.4</version>
  </dependency>
  <!-- Model Mapper -->
  <dependency>
    <groupId>org.modelmapper.extensions</groupId>
    <artifactId>modelmapper-spring</artifactId>
    <version>2.3.9</version>
  </dependency>
  ...
</dependencies>
```

Change the settings in application.properties. The part where the background color is changed is the modified part.

[application.properties]

```properties
# DataSource
spring.datasource.url=jdbc:h2:mem:testdb;DB_CLOSE_DELAY=-1;DB_CLOSE_ON_EXIT=FALSE
spring.datasource.driver-class-name=org.h2.Driver
spring.datasouce.username=sa
spring.datasouce.password=
spring.datasource.sql-script-encoding=UTF-8
spring.datasource.initialize=true
spring.datasource.schema=classpath:schema.sql
spring.datasource.data=classpath:data.sql

# H2DB
spring.h2.console.enabled=true

# message
spring.messages.basename=i18n/messages,i18n/ValidationMessages

# MyBatis
mybatis.mapper-locations=classpath*:/mapper/h2/*.xml

# Log Level
logging.level.com.example=debug
```

Point: mybatis.mapper-locations

Specify the path of the xml file in the mybatis.mapper-locations property.

This setting allows you to switch between SQL files for each database product. For example, separate SQL files for Oracle and SQL Server. Later, use this property to change the path of the xml file that you want to read.

In the sample code, all xml under "src/main/resources/mapper/h2" is targeted.

Note: Setting the Logging Level

If you want to change the logging level in Spring Boot, set the properties as follows:

[How to change the log level]

```
logging.level.package name=log level
```

The sample code changes the log level in the com.example package to debug. By setting the log level to debug, SQL executed by MyBatis is output to the log.

Modify the SQL to add the table. The part where the background color is changed is the modified part.
[schema.sql]

```sql
CREATE TABLE IF NOT EXISTS employee (
id VARCHAR(50) PRIMARY KEY,
name VARCHAR(50),
age INT
);

/* User master */
CREATE TABLE IF NOT EXISTS m_user (
  user_id VARCHAR(50) PRIMARY KEY
, password VARCHAR(100)
, user_name VARCHAR(50)
, birthday DATE
, age INT
, gender INT
, department_id INT
, role VARCHAR(50)
);

/* Department master */
CREATE TABLE IF NOT EXISTS m_department (
  department_id INT PRIMARY KEY
, department_name VARCHAR(50)
);
```

```
/* Salary table */
CREATE TABLE IF NOT EXISTS t_salary (
  user_id VARCHAR(50)
, year_month VARCHAR(50)
, salary INT
, PRIMARY KEY(user_id, year_month)
);
```

Modify the data input SQL to add the initial data. The part where the background color is changed is the modified part.

[data.sql]

```
INSERT INTO employee (id, name, age)
VALUES('1', 'Tom', 30);

/* User master */
INSERT INTO m_user (
  user_id
, password
, user_name
, birthday
, age
, gender
, department_id
, role
) VALUES
('system@co.jp', 'password', 'System Administrator', '2000-01-01', 21, 1, 1, 'ROLE_ADMIN')
, ('user@co.jp', 'password', 'User1', '2000-01-01', 21, 2, 2, 'ROLE_GENERAL')
;

/* Department master */
INSERT INTO m_department (
  department_id
, department_name
) VALUES
(1, 'System Management')
, (2, 'Sales')
;

/* Salary table */
INSERT INTO t_salary (
  user_id
, year_month
, salary
) VALUES
('user@co.jp', '11/2020', 2800)
, ('user@co.jp', '12/2020', 2900)
, ('user@co.jp', '01/2021', 3000)
;
```

Create an entity class for the user master table.

[MUser.java]

```java
package com.example.domain.user.model;

import java.util.Date;

import lombok.Data;

@Data
public class MUser {
    private String userId;
    private String password;
    private String userName;
    private Date birthday;
    private Integer age;
    private Integer gender;
    private Integer departmentId;
    private String role;
}
```

Create a repository for the user master table.

[UserMapper.java]

```java
package com.example.repository;

import org.apache.ibatis.annotations.Mapper;

import com.example.domain.user.model.MUser;

@Mapper
public interface UserMapper {

    /** User signup */
    public int insertOne(MUser user);
}
```

Point: @Mapper

To create a repository in MyBatis, annotate the Java interface with @Mapper.

Next, write the SQL in the xml file.

[UserMapper.xml]

```xml
<?xml version="1.0" encoding="UTF-8"?>
<!DOCTYPE mapper PUBLIC "-//mybatis.org//DTD Mapper 3.0//EN"
  "http://mybatis.org/dtd/mybatis-3-mapper.dtd">
```

```
<!-- Mapper and xml mapping -->
<mapper namespace="com.example.repository.UserMapper">

<!-- user registration -->
<insert id="insertOne">
    insert into m_user(
        user_id
        , password
        , user_name
        , birthday
        , age
        , gender
        , department_id
        , role
    )
    values (
        #{userId}
        , #{password}
        , #{userName}
        , #{birthday}
        , #{age}
        , #{gender}
        , #{departmentId}
        , #{role}
    )
</insert>
</mapper>
```

Point 1: Mapper-xml Mapping

You must first map the Mapper (Java interface) to the xml file. In the "mapper" tag, map the Mapper and xml. Specify the Mapper interface name in the "namespace" attribute of the "mapper" tag.

[UserMapper.xml]

```
<mapper namespace="com.example.repository.UserMapper">
```

Specify a name in the "namespace" attribute, including the package name.

Point 2: SQL-Method Mapping

Next, map the SQL and Mapper methods. This specifies the Mapper method name in the "id" attribute such as the "insert" tag. Explaining with the sample code, the part where the background color has changed below must match.

[UserMapper.java]

```
/** User signup */
public int insertOne(MUser user);
```

[UserMapper.xml]

```
<!-- user registration -->
<insert id="insertOne">
```

Point 3: Mapping method arguments to SQL parameters

Then, put the Mapper method's arguments in the SQL parameters. It can be specified in the form #{method-argument-name}. In the sample code, the method argument is the MUser class. Specify the field name in the MUser class in SQL.

[MUser.java]

```java
public class MUser {
    private String userId;
    private String password;
    private String userName;
    private Date birthday;
    private Integer age;
    private Integer gender;
    private Integer departmentId;
    private String role;
}
```

[UserMapper.xml]

```xml
<!-- user registration -->
<insert id="insertOne">
    insert into m_user(
        user_id
        , password
        , user_name
        , birthday
        , age
        , gender
        , department_id
        , role
    )
    values (
        #{userId}
        , #{password}
```

```
    , #{userName}
    , #{birthday}
    , #{age}
    , #{gender}
    , #{departmentId}
    , #{role}
  )
</insert>
```

Next, create an interface for the user service.

[UserService.java]

```java
package com.example.domain.user.service;

import com.example.domain.user.model.MUser;

public interface UserService {

  /** User signup */
  public void signup(MUser user);
}
```

Create an implementation class for the user service. From this class, call the Mapper method.

[UserServiceImpl.java]

```java
package com.example.domain.user.service.impl;

import org.springframework.beans.factory.annotation.Autowired;
import org.springframework.stereotype.Service;

import com.example.domain.user.model.MUser;
import com.example.domain.user.service.UserService;
import com.example.repository.UserMapper;

@Service
public class UserServiceImpl implements UserService {

  @Autowired
  private UserMapper mapper;

  /** User signup */
  @Override
  public void signup(MUser user) {
    user.setDepartmentId(1);
    user.setRole("ROLE_GENERAL");
    mapper.insertOne(user);
  }
```

```
}
```

Next, register ModelMapper as a bean.

[JavaConfig.java]

```java
package com.example.config;

import org.modelmapper.ModelMapper;
import org.springframework.context.annotation.Bean;
import org.springframework.context.annotation.Configuration;

@Configuration
public class JavaConfig {

  @Bean
  public ModelMapper modelMapper() {
    return new ModelMapper();
  }
}
```

Finally, modify the Signup Controller. The part where the background color is changed is the modified part.

[SignupController.java]

```java
package com.example.controller;

import java.util.Locale;
import java.util.Map;

import org.modelmapper.ModelMapper;
import org.springframework.beans.factory.annotation.Autowired;
import org.springframework.stereotype.Controller;
import org.springframework.ui.Model;
import org.springframework.validation.BindingResult;
import org.springframework.validation.annotation.Validated;
import org.springframework.web.bind.annotation.GetMapping;
import org.springframework.web.bind.annotation.ModelAttribute;
import org.springframework.web.bind.annotation.PostMapping;
import org.springframework.web.bind.annotation.RequestMapping;

import com.example.application.service.UserApplicationService;
import com.example.domain.user.model.MUser;
import com.example.domain.user.service.UserService;
import com.example.form.GroupOrder;
import com.example.form.SignupForm;

import lombok.extern.slf4j.Slf4j;

@Controller
@RequestMapping("/user")
```

```
@Slf4j
public class SignupController {

    @Autowired
    private UserApplicationService userApplicationService;

    @Autowired
    private UserService userService;

    @Autowired
    private ModelMapper modelMapper;

    /** Display the user signup screen */
    @GetMapping("/signup")
    public String getSignup(Model model, Locale locale,
            @ModelAttribute SignupForm form) {
        ...(Omitted)
    }

    /** User signup process */
    @PostMapping("/signup")
    public String postSignup(Model model, Locale locale,
            @ModelAttribute @Validated(GroupOrder.class) SignupForm form,
            BindingResult bindingResult) {

        // Input check result
        if (bindingResult.hasErrors()) {
            // NG: Return to the user signup screen
            return getSignup(model, locale, form);
        }

        log.info(form.toString());

        // Convert form to MUser class
        MUser user = modelMapper.map(form, MUser.class);

        // user signup
        userService.signup(user);

        // Redirect to login screen
        return "redirect:/login";
    }
}
```

Point: ModelMapper

You can easily copy the contents of a field using the map method of ModelMapper. To copy a field, the source and destination field names must match.

Note: Do Not Pass Form Classes to Services

The SignupForm and MUser classes have the same fields. There are two reasons to copy form class values:

- Changes in the screen do not require service modification.
- The service can be reused from other screens.

Let's compare the case where SignupForm is used as an argument of the service and the case where it is not.

[When the SignupForm class is used as an argument]

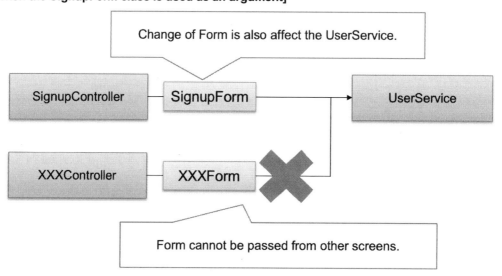

[When using the MUser class as an argument]

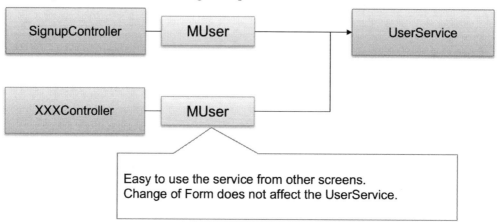

When creating a service, keep this design in mind.

Execution

Run Spring Boot and access the following URL.

[URL]
http://localhost:8080/user/signup

Let's register a user.
[User signup screen]

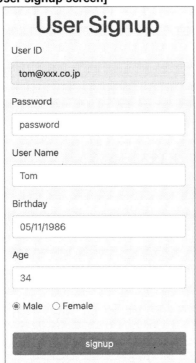

If no error occurs, the user will be registered. In addition, the following log is output.

[Log] (Excerpt)

```
==> Preparing: insert into m_user( user_id , password , user_name , birthday , age , gender ,
department_id , role ) values ( ? , ? , ? , ? , ? , ? , ? , ? )
==> Parameters: tom@xxx.co.jp(String), password(String), tom(String), 1986-11-05
00:00:00.0(Timestamp), 34(Integer), 1(Integer), 1(Integer), ROLE_GENERAL(String)
<==    Updates: 1
```

These are MyBatis logs, and the following contents are output.

- Execution SQL
- Value of the parameter passed to SQL
- Number of data updates

You can also check whether it is actually registered in the database or by using the H2 database console.

[H2 Console URL]

http://localhost:8080/h2-console

Check the contents of the M_USER table.

[H2 Console Screen]

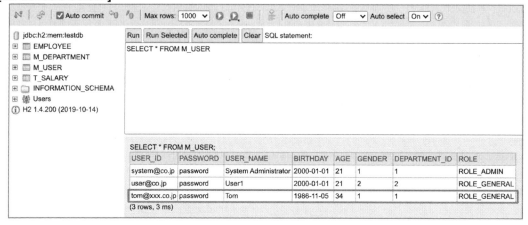

The user is registered.

8.2.2 select…multiple records

Overview

Displays all data of the user master on the user list screen.

[Execution result]

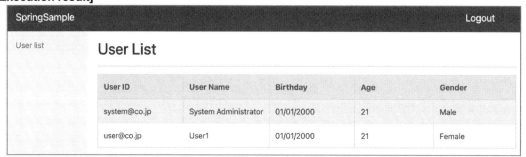

Directory

There is no change in the directory structure.

Source Code

First, set the properties. The part where the background color is changed is the modified part.

[application.properties]

```
# DataSource
spring.datasource.url=jdbc:h2:mem:testdb;DB_CLOSE_DELAY=-1;DB_CLOSE_ON_EXIT=FALSE
spring.datasource.driver-class-name=org.h2.Driver
spring.datasouce.username=sa
spring.datasouce.password=
spring.datasource.sql-script-encoding=UTF-8
spring.datasource.initialize=true
spring.datasource.schema=classpath:schema.sql
spring.datasource.data=classpath:data.sql

# H2DB
spring.h2.console.enabled=true

# message
spring.messages.basename=i18n/messages,i18n/ValidationMessages

# MyBatis
mybatis.mapper-locations=classpath*:/mapper/h2/*.xml
mybatis.configuration.map-underscore-to-camel-case=true
mybatis.type-aliases-package=com.example.domain.user.model

# Log Level
logging.level.com.example=debug
```

These settings will be explained later.

Next, add a method to the mapper that gets multiple users. The part where the background color is changed is the modified part.

[UserMapper.java]

```java
package com.example.repository;

import java.util.List;

import org.apache.ibatis.annotations.Mapper;

import com.example.domain.user.model.MUser;

@Mapper
public interface UserMapper {

    /** User signup */
    public int insertOne(MUser user);

    /** Get user */
```

```
   public List<MUser> findMany();
}
```

Point: Multiple select

If the return value of the select statement is multiple records, set the return value of the method to List.

Then modify the xml file. The part where the background color is changed is the modified part.

[UserMapper.xml]

```xml
<?xml version="1.0" encoding="UTF-8"?>
<!DOCTYPE mapper PUBLIC "-//mybatis.org//DTD Mapper 3.0//EN"
 "http://mybatis.org/dtd/mybatis-3-mapper.dtd">

<!-- Mapper and xml mapping -->
<mapper namespace="com.example.repository.UserMapper">

  <!-- user registration -->
  <insert id="insertOne">
    ...(Omitted)
  </insert>

  <!-- Get user(multiple) -->
  <select id="findMany" resultType="MUser">
    select
        *
    from
        m_user
  </select>
</mapper>
```

Point: select tag

To write a select statement, use the select tag. The "resultType" attribute specifies the data type of the return value. If there is only one column in the select result, integer(int) and string can also be specified as the return value.

When specifying the MUser type as the return value as in the sample code, it is convenient to make the following settings.

[application.properties]

```
mybatis.configuration.map-underscore-to-camel-case=true
mybatis.type-aliases-package=com.example.domain.user.model
```

- **mybatis.configuration.map-underscore-to-camel-case**

Setting this property to true converts underscores in select results to camelcases. For example, assume that the column name in the select result is "user_id". In that case, "user_id" is mapped to the "userId" of the Java class.

- **mybatis.type-aliases-package**
  If you specify a data type such as MUser for resultType, you must also include the package name. However, you can omit the package name that you set in mybatis.type-aliases-package.

[application.properties]

```
mybatis.type-aliases-package=com.example.domain.user.model
```

[UserMapper.xml]

```
<select id="findMany" resultType="MUser">
```

The next step is to modify the user service. The part where the background color is changed is the modified part.

[UserService.java]

```java
package com.example.domain.user.service;

import java.util.List;

import com.example.domain.user.model.MUser;

public interface UserService {

    /** User signup */
    public void signup(MUser user);

    /** Get user */
    public List<MUser> getUsers();
}
```

You also modify the implementation classes for user services. The part where the background color is changed is the modified part.

[UserServiceImpl.java]

```java
@Service
public class UserServiceImpl implements UserService {

    @Autowired
    private UserMapper mapper;
```

```java
/** User signup */
@Override
public void signup(MUser user) {
    ...(Omitted)
}

/** Get user */
@Override
public List<MUser> getUsers() {
    return mapper.findMany();
}
}
```

Modify the user list controller. The part where the background color is changed is the modified part.

[UserListController.java]

```java
package com.example.controller;

import java.util.List;

import org.springframework.beans.factory.annotation.Autowired;
import org.springframework.stereotype.Controller;
import org.springframework.ui.Model;
import org.springframework.web.bind.annotation.GetMapping;
import org.springframework.web.bind.annotation.RequestMapping;

import com.example.domain.user.model.MUser;
import com.example.domain.user.service.UserService;

@Controller
@RequestMapping("/user")
public class UserListController {

    @Autowired
    private UserService userService;

    /** Display user list screen */
    @GetMapping("/list")
    public String getUserList(Model model) {

        // Get user list
        List<MUser> userList = userService.getUsers();

        // Registered in Model
        model.addAttribute("userList", userList);

        // Display user list screen
        return "user/list";
    }
}
```

The list of users is retrieved from the user service and the result is registered in Model.

Finally, modify the screen to display the user list. The part where the background color is changed is the modified part.

[list.html]

```html
<!DOCTYPE html>
<html xmlns:th="http://www.thymeleaf.org"
  xmlns:layout="http://www.ultraq.net.nz/thymeleaf/layout"
  layout:decorate="~{layout/layout}">
<head>
 <title>User List</title>
 <!-- Read Dedicated CSS -->
 <link rel="stylesheet" th:href="@{/css/user/list.css}">
</head>
<body>
 <div layout:fragment="content">
  <div class="header border-bottom">
   <h1 class="h2">User List</h1>
  </div>
  <!-- List display -->
  <div>
   <table class="table table-striped table-bordered table-hover">
    <thead class="thead-light">
     <tr>
      <th class="th-width">User ID</th>
      <th class="th-width">User Name</th>
      <th class="th-width">Birthday</th>
      <th class="th-width">Age</th>
      <th class="th-width">Gender</th>
     </tr>
    </thead>
    <tbody>
     <tr th:each="item: ${userList}">
      <td th:text="${item.userId}"></td>
      <td th:text="${item.userName}"></td>
      <td th:text="${#dates.format(item.birthday, 'dd/MM/YYYY')}"></td>
      <td th:text="${item.age}"></td>
      <td th:text="${item.gender == 1} ? 'Male': 'Female'"></td>
     </tr>
    </tbody>
   </table>
  </div>
 </div>
</body>
</html>
```

> **Note: Trinomial**
>
> Java trinomials can also be used in the th attribute. Explaining with sample code, it is the following part.
>
> **[list.html]**
>
> ```
> <td th:text="${item.gender == 1} ? 'Male': 'Female'"></td>
> ```
>
> This code shows "male" if the gender value is 1, and "female" otherwise.

Execution

Run Spring Boot and access the following URL.

[URL]
http://localhost:8080/user/list

[User list screen]

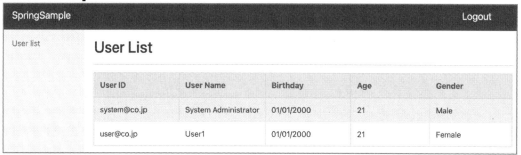

Displays all user master data.

8.2.3 select...1 record

Overview

From the user list, display the details of the selected user on another screen.

[Screen Transition]

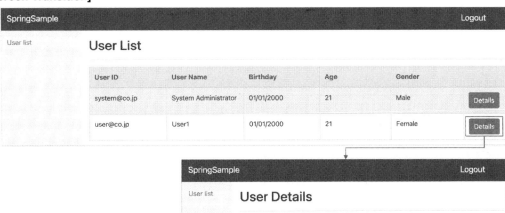

Directory

The directory structure is as follows. The part where the background color is changed is the new part to be added.

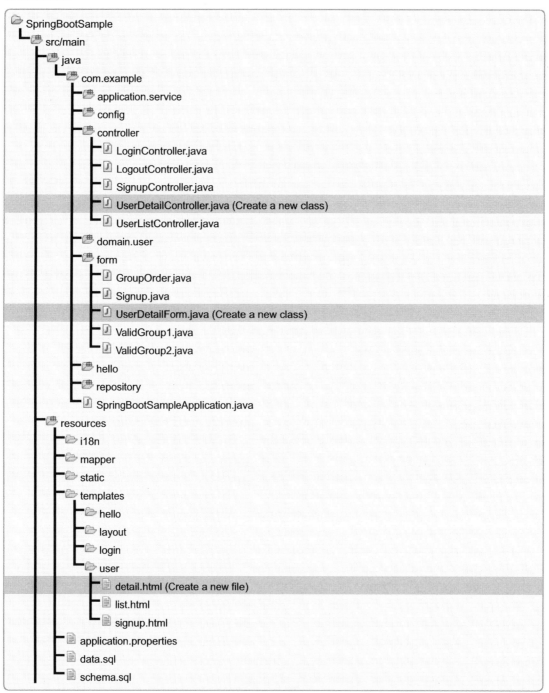

```
        L 📄 pom.xml
```

Source Code

First, modify the mapper. The part where the background color is changed is the modified part.
[UserMapper.java]

```java
@Mapper
public interface UserMapper {

    /** User signup */
    public int insertOne(MUser user);

    /** Get user */
    public List<MUser> findMany();

    /** Get user(1record) */
    public MUser findOne(String userId);
}
```

Then modify the xml file. The part where the background color is changed is the modified part.
[UserMapper.xml]

```xml
<?xml version="1.0" encoding="UTF-8"?>
<!DOCTYPE mapper PUBLIC "-//mybatis.org//DTD Mapper 3.0//EN"
 "http://mybatis.org/dtd/mybatis-3-mapper.dtd">

<!-- Mapper and xml mapping -->
<mapper namespace="com.example.repository.UserMapper">

<!-- Mapping definition (user) -->
<resultMap type="com.example.domain.user.model.MUser" id="user">
  <id column="user_id" property="userId" />
  <result column="password" property="password" />
  <result column="user_name" property="userName" />
  <result column="birthday" property="birthday" />
  <result column="age" property="age" />
  <result column="gender" property="gender" />
  <result column="department_id" property="departmentId" />
  <result column="role" property="role" />
</resultMap>

<!-- user registration -->
<insert id="insertOne">
    ...(Omitted)
</insert>
```

```
<!-- Get user(multiple) -->
<select id="findMany" resultType="User">
    …(Omitted)
</select>
```

```
<!-- Get user(1record) -->
<select id="findOne" resultMap="user">
    select
        *
    from
        m_user
    where
        user_id = #{userId}
</select>
</mapper>
```

Point 1: resultMap tag

The resultMap tag is used to map the Java class to the select result. Use the resultMap tag, especially when executing complex select statements.

The type attribute contains the class name, including the package name. The id attribute can have any value.

In the resultMap tag, set the mapping between the select result and the Java class. First, prepare an id tag or a result tag. Set the following attributes within those tags:

Attribute	Description
column	Sets the column name of the select result
property	Sets the field name of the Java class.

The following explains the difference between the id and result tags. The id tag is a required tag. Because the List of return values contains as many data as the number of values in the id tag. For example, suppose you get a select result like this:

[Example: id tag]

Select result

user_id	user_name
user@co.jp	user1
user@co.jp	user1

Return value List<MUser>

index	userId	userName
1	user@co.jp	user1

There are two select results, but the only "user_id" values set for the id tags are "user@co.jp". In that case, the List<MUser> returned by the mapper contains only one piece of data.

That is, the return value is made so that the column value set in the id tag is unique. This idea is required for table joins. You will create a sample table join later in this chapter.

Point 2: Mapping of Select and resultMap Tags

If you use resultMap tag, add the resultMap attribute to the select tag. The value of this attribute specifies the id of the resultMap tag.

[UserMapper.xml]

```xml
<!-- Mapping definition (user) -->
<resultMap type="com.example.domain.user.model.MUser" id="user">
  ...
</resultMap>
...
<!-- Get user(1record) -->
<select id="findOne" resultMap="user">
  ...
</select>
```

Then modify the user service. The part where the background color is changed is the modified part.
[UserService.java]

```java
public interface UserService {

    /** User signup */
    public void signup(MUser user);

    /** Get user */
    public List<MUser> getUsers();

    /** Get user(1record) */
    public MUser getUserOne(String userId);
}
```

Also modify the user service implementation class. The part where the background color is changed is the modified part.
[UserServiceImpl.java]

```java
@Service
public class UserServiceImpl implements UserService {

    @Autowired
    private UserMapper mapper;
```

```
    /** User signup */
    @Override
    public void signup(MUser user) {
        ...(Omitted)
    }

    /** Get user */
    @Override
    public List<MUser> getUsers() {
        return mapper.findMany();
    }

    /** Get user(1record) */
    @Override
    public MUser getUserOne(String userId) {
        return mapper.findOne(userId);
    }
}
```

Next, create a form class for the user detail.

[UserDetailForm.java]

```
package com.example.form;

import java.util.Date;

import lombok.Data;

@Data
public class UserDetailForm {
    private String userId;
    private String password;
    private String userName;
    private Date birthday;
    private Integer age;
    private Integer gender;
}
```

Next, add a link so that you can move from the user list screen to the user details screen. The part where the background color is changed is the modified part.

[list.html]

```
<!DOCTYPE html>
<html xmlns:th="http://www.thymeleaf.org"
  xmlns:layout="http://www.ultraq.net.nz/thymeleaf/layout"
  layout:decorate="~{layout/layout}">
<head>
  <title>User List</title>
  <!-- Read Dedicated CSS -->
```

```
 <link rel="stylesheet" th:href="@{/css/user/list.css}">
</head>
<body>
 <div layout:fragment="content">
  <div class="header border-bottom">
   <h1 class="h2">User List</h1>
  </div>
  <!-- List display -->
  <div>
   <table class="table table-striped table-bordered table-hover">
    <thead class="thead-light">
     <tr>
      <th class="th-width">User ID</th>
      <th class="th-width">User Name</th>
      <th class="th-width">Birthday</th>
      <th class="th-width">Age</th>
      <th class="th-width">Gender</th>
      <th></th>
     </tr>
    </thead>
    <tbody>
     <tr th:each="item: ${userList}">
      <td th:text="${item.userId}"></td>
      <td th:text="${item.userName}"></td>
      <td th:text="${#dates.format(item.birthday, 'dd/MM/YYYY')}"></td>
      <td th:text="${item.age}"></td>
      <td th:text="${item.gender == 1} ? 'Male': 'Female'"></td>
      <td>
       <a class="btn btn-primary" th:href="@{/user/detail/' + ${item.userId}}">
        Details
       </a>
      </td>
     </tr>
    </tbody>
   </table>
  </div>
 </div>
</body>
</html>
```

Point: Dynamic URL

You can also combine strings in the th attribute. If you enclose it in single quotes like the sample code, it will be a fixed character string. And you can use the plus sign to combine strings.

The sample code generates the URL "/user/detail/(user ID)".

Create a controller for the user detail.

[UserDetailController.java]

```java
package com.example.controller;

import org.modelmapper.ModelMapper;
import org.springframework.beans.factory.annotation.Autowired;
import org.springframework.stereotype.Controller;
import org.springframework.ui.Model;
import org.springframework.web.bind.annotation.GetMapping;
import org.springframework.web.bind.annotation.PathVariable;
import org.springframework.web.bind.annotation.RequestMapping;

import com.example.domain.user.model.MUser;
import com.example.domain.user.service.UserService;
import com.example.form.UserDetailForm;

@Controller
@RequestMapping("/user")
public class UserDetailController {

    @Autowired
    private UserService userService;

    @Autowired
    private ModelMapper modelMapper;

    /** Display user details screen */
    @GetMapping("/detail/{userId:.+}")
    public String getUser(UserDetailForm form, Model model,
            @PathVariable("userId") String userId) {

        // Get user
        MUser user = userService.getUserOne(userId);
        user.setPassword(null);

        // Get user
        form = modelMapper.map(user, UserDetailForm.class);

        // Registered in Model
        model.addAttribute("userDetailForm", form);

        // Display user details screen
        return "user/detail";
    }
}
```

Point: Dynamic URL

Use a dynamic URL to receive part of the URL. To do this, put the {variable name} in the URL.

The @PathVariable annotation is used to receive the value of a variable in a URL. The value of this annotation specifies the name of a variable in the URL.

[How to receive a dynamic URL]

```
/** Display user details screen */
@GetMapping("/detail/{userId:.+}")
public String getUser(UserDetailForm form, Model model,
     @PathVariable("userId") String userId) {
```

In the sample application in this book, the user ID is in the form of an email address. Therefore, "/detail/{userId}" may not be enough to receive the value. For example, if the value "user@xxx.co.jp" is passed, only "user@xxx.co" will be received. We are using a regular expression in order to respond to it. Therefore, the URL is set to "/detail/{userId:.+}". If it is not in the email address format, "/detail/{userId}" is fine.

Finally, create a user details screen.

[detail.html]

```html
<!DOCTYPE html>
<html xmlns:th="http://www.thymeleaf.org"
 xmlns:layout="http://www.ultraq.net.nz/thymeleaf/layout"
 layout:decorate="~{layout/layout}">
<head>
 <title>User Details</title>
 <!-- Read CSS -->
 <link rel="stylesheet" th:href="@{/css/user/list.css}">
</head>
<body>
 <div layout:fragment="content">
  <div class="header border-bottom">
   <h1 class="h2">User Details</h1>
  </div>
  <form id="user-detail-form" method="post" th:action="@{/user/detail}"
    class="form-signup" th:object="${userDetailForm}">
   <!-- User Details information -->
   <table class="table table-striped table-bordered table-hover">
    <tbody>
     <tr>
      <th class="w-25">User ID</th>
      <td th:text="*{userId}"></td>
     </tr>
     <tr>
      <th>Password</th>
      <td>
       <input type="text" class="form-control" th:field="*{password}"/>
      </td>
     </tr>
     <tr>
```

153

```html
      <th>User Name</th>
      <td>
       <input type="text" class="form-control" th:field="*{userName}"/>
      </td>
     </tr>
     <tr>
      <th>Birthday</th>
      <td th:text="*{#dates.format(birthday, 'dd/MM/YYYY')}"></td>
     </tr>
     <tr>
      <th>Age</th>
      <td th:text="*{age}"></td>
     </tr>
     <tr>
      <th>Gender</th>
      <td th:text="*{gender == 1 ? 'Male': 'Female'}"></td>
     </tr>
    </tbody>
   </table>
  </form>
 </div>
</body>
</html>
```

Execution

Run Spring Boot and access the following URL.

[URL]
http://localhost:8080/user/list

Click the Detail button on the user list screen. Moves to the user detail screen.

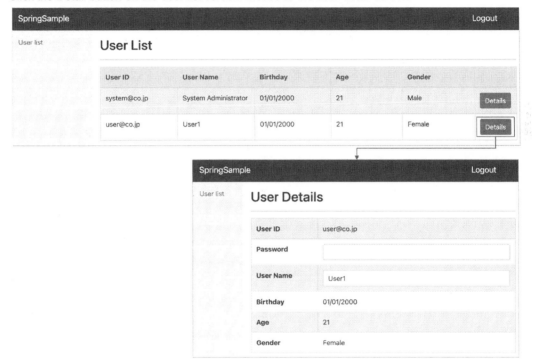

8.2.4 update/delete

Overview

Allows you to update user master data from the user details screen. Add "delete" and "update" buttons to the user details screen.

[User detail screen]

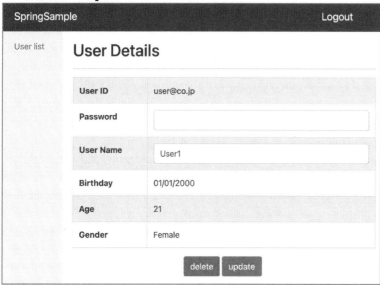

Directory

There is no change in the directory structure.

Source Code

First, modify the mapper. The part where the background color is changed is the modified part.
[UserMapper.java]

```java
package com.example.repository;

import java.util.List;

import org.apache.ibatis.annotations.Mapper;
import org.apache.ibatis.annotations.Param;

import com.example.domain.user.model.MUser;
```

```
@Mapper
public interface UserMapper {

    /** User signup */
    public int insertOne(MUser user);

    /** Get user */
    public List<MUser> findMany();

    /** Get user(1record) */
    public MUser findOne(String userId);

    /** Update user */
    public void updateOne(@Param("userId") String userId,
        @Param("password") String password,
        @Param("userName") String userName);

    /** Delete user */
    public int deleteOne(@Param("userId") String userId);
}
```

Point: @Param

If you use more than one parameter, annotate the method arguments with @Param. The value of this annotation specifies the parameter name.

Then modify the xml file. The part where the background color is changed is the modified part.

[UserMapper.xml]

```
<?xml version="1.0" encoding="UTF-8"?>
<!DOCTYPE mapper PUBLIC "-//mybatis.org//DTD Mapper 3.0//EN"
  "http://mybatis.org/dtd/mybatis-3-mapper.dtd">

<!-- Mapper and xml mapping -->
<mapper namespace="com.example.repository.UserMapper">

  <!-- Mapping definition (user) -->
  <resultMap type="com.example.domain.user.model.MUser" id="user">
      ...(Omitted)
  </resultMap>

  <!-- user registration -->
  <insert id="insertOne">
      ...(Omitted)
  </insert>

  <!-- Get user(multiple) -->
  <select id="findMany" resultType="MUser">
```

```
    …(Omitted)
  </select>

  <!-- Get user(1record) -->
  <select id="findOne" resultMap="user">
    …(Omitted)
  </select>

  <!-- Update user -->
  <update id="updateOne">
    update
      m_user
    set
      password = #{password}
      , user_name = #{userName}
    where
      user_id = #{userId}
  </update>

  <!-- Delete user -->
  <delete id="deleteOne">
    delete from
      m_user
    where
      user_id = #{userId}
  </delete>
</mapper>
```

Point: Embedding @Param

Values specified with the @Param annotation can be embedded in SQL. Specify #{parameter name} to embed as a parameter in SQL. This allows you to map method arguments to parameters in SQL.

Note: When the MUser type is used as an argument

You can also specify a data type such as MUser instead of the method argument of type int or String. In that case, specify # {parameter name.field name}.

Example: If the UserMapper argument is changed to MUser type
[UserMapper.java]

```
public void updateOne(@Param("user") MUser user);
```

[UserMapper.xml]

```
<update id="updateOne">
```

```
update
    m_user
set
    password = #{user.password}
    , user_name = #{user.userName}
where
    user_id = #{user.userId}
</update>
```

Then modify the user service. The part where the background color is changed is the modified part.

[UserService.java]

```java
public interface UserService {

    /** User signup */
    public void signup(MUser user);

    /** Get user */
    public List<MUser> getUsers();

    /** Get user(1record) */
    public MUser getUserOne(String userId);

    /** Update user */
    public void updateUserOne(String userId,
        String password,
        String userName);

    /** Delete user */
    public void deleteUserOne(String userId);
}
```

Also modify the user service implementation class. The part where the background color is changed is the modified part.

[UserServiceImpl.java]

```java
@Service
public class UserServiceImpl implements UserService {

    @Autowired
    private UserMapper mapper;

    /** User signup */
    @Override
    public void signup(MUser user) {
        …(Omitted)
    }
```

```java
    /** Get user */
    @Override
    public List<MUser> getUsers() {
        return mapper.findMany();
    }

    /** Get user(1record) */
    @Override
    public MUser getUserOne(String userId) {
        return mapper.findOne(userId);
    }

    /** Update user */
    @Override
    public void updateUserOne(String userId,
            String password,
            String userName) {
        mapper.updateOne(userId, password, userName);
    }

    /** Delete user */
    @Override
    public void deleteUserOne(String userId) {
        int count = mapper.deleteOne(userId);
    }
}
```

Then modify the controller on the user details screen. The part where the background color is changed is the modified part.

[UserDetailController.java]

```java
@Controller
@RequestMapping("/user")
public class UserDetailController {

    @Autowired
    private UserService userService;

    @Autowired
    private ModelMapper modelMapper;

    /** Display user details screen */
    @GetMapping("/detail/{userId:.+}")
    public String getUser(UserDetailForm form, Model model,
            @PathVariable("userId") String userId) {
        …(Omitted)
    }

    /** User update process */
```

```java
@PostMapping(value = "/detail", params = "update")
public String updateUser(UserDetailForm form, Model model) {
    // Update user
    userService.updateUserOne(form.getUserId(),
            form.getPassword(),
            form.getUserName());

    // Redirect to user list screen
    return "redirect:/user/list";
}

/** User delete process */
@PostMapping(value = "/detail", params = "delete")
public String deleteUser(UserDetailForm form, Model model) {
    // Delete user
    userService.deleteUserOne(form.getUserId());

    // Redirect to user list screen
    return "redirect:/user/list";
}
}
```

Point: params attribute

Set the params attribute in @PostMapping. For this attribute, specify the same value as the name attribute of the button tag. By doing this, you can change the method received by the controller even if the buttons are in the same form tag.

By the way, set the URL in the value attribute.

Finally, modify the user details screen. The part where the background color is changed is the modified part.

[detail.html]

```html
<!DOCTYPE html>
<html xmlns:th="http://www.thymeleaf.org"
 xmlns:layout="http://www.ultraq.net.nz/thymeleaf/layout"
 layout:decorate="~{layout/layout}">
<head>
 <title>User Details</title>
 <!-- Read CSS -->
 <link rel="stylesheet" th:href="@{/css/user/list.css}">
</head>
<body>
 <div layout:fragment="content">
  <div class="header border-bottom">
   <h1 class="h2">User Details</h1>
  </div>
  <form id="user-detail-form" method="post" th:action="@{/user/detail}"
     class="form-signup" th:object="${userDetailForm}">
```

```
    <input type="hidden" th:field="*{userId}" />
    <!-- User Details information -->
    <table class="table table-striped table-bordered table-hover">
      …(Omitted)
    </table>
    <!-- Button area -->
    <div class="text-center">
      <!-- Delete button -->
      <button class="btn btn-danger" type="submit" name="delete">
        delete
      </button>
      <!-- Update button -->
      <button class="btn btn-primary" type="submit" name="update">
        update
      </button>
    </div>
  </form>
 </div>
</body>
</html>
```

Execution

Run SpringBoot and access the user details screen. Please change a user name and press the "update" button. You will be redirected to the user list screen to see the changed user name.

Click the "delete" button to delete the user.

8.3 MyBatis advanced

From here, you will learn how to use MyBatis in an applied manner.

- Dynamic SQL
- Mapping to Nested Objects
- Table join (one-to-many)

8.3.1 Dynamic SQL

Overview

Modify the user list screen so that users can be searched.

[User list screen]

Dynamically changes the where clause of a select statement, depending on what is entered on the screen, as follows:

No	User ID	User name	SQL
1	Not input	Not input	Search all
2	Input	Not input	Filter by user ID
3	Not input	Input	Filter by user name
4	Input	Input	Filter by user ID and user name

Note that both user IDs and user names are partial match searches.

Directory

The directory structure is as follows. The part where the background color is changed is the new part to be added.

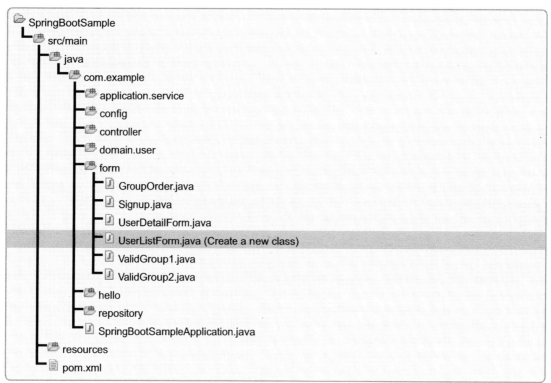

Source Code

First, modify the mapper. The part where the background color is changed is the modified part.
[UserMapper.java]

```java
@Mapper
public interface UserMapper {

    /** User signup */
    public int insertOne(MUser user);

    /** Get user */
    public List<MUser> findMany(MUser user);

    /** Get user(1record) */
    public MUser findOne(String userId);
```

```
/** Update user */
public void updateOne(@Param("userId") String userId,
      @Param("password") String password,
      @Param("userName") String userName);

/** Delete user */
public int deleteOne(@Param("userId") String userId);
}
```

Then modify xml. The part where the background color is changed is the modified part.

[UserMapper.xml]

```xml
<?xml version="1.0" encoding="UTF-8"?>
<!DOCTYPE mapper PUBLIC "-//mybatis.org//DTD Mapper 3.0//EN"
 "http://mybatis.org/dtd/mybatis-3-mapper.dtd">

<!-- Mapper and xml mapping -->
<mapper namespace="com.example.repository.UserMapper">

  <!-- Mapping definition (user) -->
  <resultMap type="com.example.domain.user.model.MUser" id="user">
    ...(Omitted)
  </resultMap>

  <!-- user registration -->
  <insert id="insertOne">
    ...(Omitted)
  </insert>

  <!-- Get user(multiple) -->
  <select id="findMany" resultType="MUser">
    select
      *
    from
      m_user
    <where>
     <if test="userId != null">
       user_id like '%' || #{userId} || '%'
     </if>
     <if test="userName != null">
       and user_name like '%' || #{userName} || '%'
     </if>
    </where>
  </select>

  <!-- Get user(1record) -->
  <select id="findOne" resultMap="user">
    ...(Omitted)
  </select>
```

```
<!-- Update user -->
<update id="updateOne">
    ...(Omitted)
</update>

<!-- Delete user -->
<delete id="deleteOne">
    ...(Omitted)
</delete>
</mapper>
```

Point 1: if tag

Use this if tag to generate dynamic SQL. The usage is the same as the Java if statement. Write a conditional expression in the test attribute. If the result of the conditional expression is true, the SQL in this tag will be added. If the result is false, no SQL will be added.

Point 2: where tag

If even one if tag in the where tag is true, add a where clause. That is, use this tag when you are not sure if you always use the where clause. If you use SQL that always uses the where clause, use only the if tag.

Then modify the user service. The part where the background color is changed is the modified part.

[UserService.java]

```java
public interface UserService {

    /** User signup */
    public void signup(MUser user);

    /** Get user */
    public List<MUser> getUsers(MUser user);

    /** Get user(1record) */
    public MUser getUserOne(String userId);

    /** Update user */
    public void updateUserOne(String userId,
        String password,
        String userName);

    /** Delete user */
    public void deleteUserOne(String userId);
}
```

Also modify the user service implementation class. The part where the background color is changed is the modified part.

[UserServiceImpl.java]

```java
@Service
public class UserServiceImpl implements UserService {

    @Autowired
    private UserMapper mapper;

    /** User signup */
    @Override
    public void signup(MUser user) {
        ...(Omitted)
    }

    /** Get user */
    @Override
    public List<MUser> getUsers(MUser user) {
        return mapper.findMany(user);
    }

    /** Get user(1record) */
    @Override
    public MUser getUserOne(String userId) {
        return mapper.findOne(userId);
    }

    /** Update user */
    @Override
    public void updateUserOne(String userId,
            String password,
            String userName) {
        mapper.updateOne(userId, password, userName);
    }

    /** Delete user */
    @Override
    public void deleteUserOne(String userId) {
        int count = mapper.deleteOne(userId);
    }
}
```

Next, create a form class for the user list screen. It is a class to have the user search condition entered from the screen.

[UserListForm]

```java
package com.example.form;

import lombok.Data;
```

```
@Data
public class UserListForm {
    private String userId;
    private String userName;
}
```

Next, modify the controller on the user list screen. The part where the background color is changed is the modified part.

[UserListController.java]

```
package com.example.controller;

import java.util.List;

import org.modelmapper.ModelMapper;
import org.springframework.beans.factory.annotation.Autowired;
import org.springframework.stereotype.Controller;
import org.springframework.ui.Model;
import org.springframework.web.bind.annotation.GetMapping;
import org.springframework.web.bind.annotation.ModelAttribute;
import org.springframework.web.bind.annotation.PostMapping;
import org.springframework.web.bind.annotation.RequestMapping;

import com.example.domain.user.model.MUser;
import com.example.domain.user.service.UserService;
import com.example.form.UserListForm;

@Controller
@RequestMapping("/user")
public class UserListController {

    @Autowired
    private UserService userService;

    @Autowired
    private ModelMapper modelMapper;

    /** Display user list screen */
    @GetMapping("/list")
    public String getUserList(@ModelAttribute UserListForm form, Model model) {

        // Convert form to MUser class
        MUser user = modelMapper.map(form, MUser.class);

        // Get user list
        List<MUser> userList = userService.getUsers(user);

        // Registered in Model
        model.addAttribute("userList", userList);
```

```
    // Display user list screen
    return "user/list";
}

/** User search process */
@PostMapping("/list")
public String postUserList(@ModelAttribute UserListForm form, Model model) {

    // Convert form to MUser class
    MUser user = modelMapper.map(form, MUser.class);

    // Get user list
    List<MUser> userList = userService.getUsers(user);

    // Registered in Model
    model.addAttribute("userList", userList);

    // Display user list screen
    return "user/list";
    }
}
```

Finally, add a search field to the user list screen. The part where the background color is changed is the modified part.

[list.html]

```html
<!DOCTYPE html>
<html xmlns:th="http://www.thymeleaf.org"
 xmlns:layout="http://www.ultraq.net.nz/thymeleaf/layout"
 layout:decorate="~{layout/layout}">
<head>
 <title>User List</title>
 <!-- Read Dedicated CSS -->
 <link rel="stylesheet" th:href="@{/css/user/list.css}">
</head>
<body>
 <div layout:fragment="content">
  <div class="header border-bottom">
   <h1 class="h2">User List</h1>
  </div>
  <!-- Search -->
  <div class="mb-4">
   <form id="user-search-form" method="post" th:action="@{/user/list}"
     class="form-inline" th:object="${userListForm}">
    <div class="form-group" >
     <label for="userId" class="mr-2">User ID</label>
     <input type="text" class="form-control" th:field="*{userId}"/>
    </div>
    <div class="form-group mx-sm-3" >
     <label for="userName" class="mr-2">User Name</label>
```

```
    <input type="text" class="form-control" th:field="*{userName}"/>
    </div>
    <button class="btn btn-primary" type="submit">
    search
    </button>
    </form>
  </div>
  <!-- List display -->
  <div>
    <table class="table table-striped table-bordered table-hover">
      ...(Omitted)
    </table>
  </div>
  </div>
</body>
</html>
```

Execution

Run SpringBoot to access the user list screen. Enter the search criteria and click the Search button.

[User list screen] (After Search)

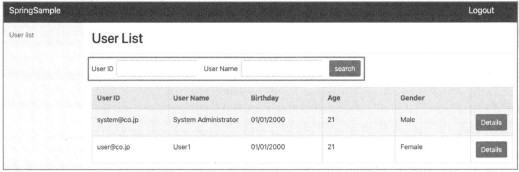

8.3.2 Mapping to Nested Objects

Overview

In this section, you will learn how to get the results of a table join. Display the department to which the user belongs on the user detail screen.

[User details screen]

The relationship between the department and the user master is as follows.

[ER diagram]

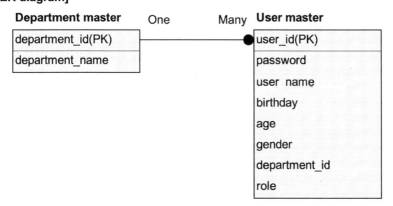

The department master and user master have a one-to-many relationship. In other words, a user can belong to only one department.

Directory

The directory structure is as follows. The part where the background color is changed is the new part to be added.

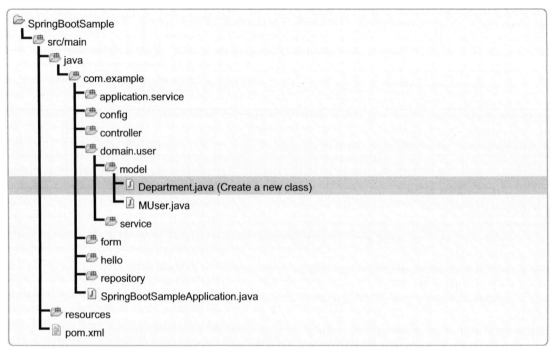

Source Code

Next, create an entity class for the department.
[Department.java]

```
package com.example.domain.user.model;

import lombok.Data;

@Data
public class Department {
    private Integer departmentId;
    private String departmentName;
}
```

Then add the department to the user entity class. The part where the background color is changed is the modified part.

[MUser.java]

```
@Data
public class MUser {
    private String userId;
    private String password;
    private String userName;
    private Date birthday;
    private Integer age;
    private Integer gender;
    private Integer departmentId;
    private String role;
    private Department department;
}
```

Add a department to the form class on the user details screen. The part where the background color is changed is the modified part.

[UserDetailForm.java]

```
package com.example.form;

import java.util.Date;

import com.example.domain.user.model.Department;

import lombok.Data;

@Data
public class UserDetailForm {
    private String userId;
    private String password;
    private String userName;
    private Date birthday;
    private Integer age;
    private Integer gender;
    private Department department;
}
```

Then modify xml. The part where the background color is changed is the modified part.

[UserMapper.xml]

```
<?xml version="1.0" encoding="UTF-8"?>
<!DOCTYPE mapper PUBLIC "-//mybatis.org//DTD Mapper 3.0//EN"
  "http://mybatis.org/dtd/mybatis-3-mapper.dtd">

<!-- Mapper and xml mapping -->
<mapper namespace="com.example.repository.UserMapper">

  <!-- Mapping definition (user) -->
```

```xml
<resultMap type="com.example.domain.user.model.MUser" id="user">
  <id column="user_id" property="userId" />
  <result column="password" property="password" />
  <result column="user_name" property="userName" />
  <result column="birthday" property="birthday" />
  <result column="age" property="age" />
  <result column="gender" property="gender" />
  <result column="department_id" property="departmentId" />
  <result column="role" property="role" />
  <association property="department" resultMap="department"/>
</resultMap>

<!-- Mapping definition (department) -->
<resultMap type="com.example.domain.user.model.Department" id="department">
  <id column="department_id" property="departmentId" />
  <result column="department_name" property="departmentName" />
</resultMap>

<!-- user registration -->
<insert id="insertOne">
    ...(Omitted)
</insert>

<!-- Get user(multiple) -->
<select id="findMany" resultType="MUser">
    ...(Omitted)
</select>

<!-- Get user(1record) -->
<select id="findOne" resultMap="user">
  select
    *
  from
    m_user
    left join m_department
      on m_user.department_id = m_department.department_id
  where
    user_id = #{userId}
</select>

<!-- Update user -->
<update id="updateOne">
    ...(Omitted)
</update>

<!-- Delete user -->
<delete id="deleteOne">
    ...(Omitted)
</delete>
</mapper>
```

174

Point: association tag

The association tag allows you to include another mapping definition in the mapping definition. In other words, it is used for table joins. However, you can use the association tag when there is only one data to join.

Then modify the user details screen. The part where the background color is changed is the modified part.

[detail.html]

```
<!DOCTYPE html>
<html xmlns:th="http://www.thymeleaf.org"
 xmlns:layout="http://www.ultraq.net.nz/thymeleaf/layout"
 layout:decorate="~{layout/layout}">
<head>
 <title>User Details</title>
 <!-- Read CSS -->
 <link rel="stylesheet" th:href="@{/css/user/list.css}">
</head>
<body>
 <div layout:fragment="content">
  <div class="header border-bottom">
   <h1 class="h2">User Details</h1>
  </div>
  <form id="user-detail-form" method="post" th:action="@{/user/detail}"
    class="form-signup" th:object="${userDetailForm}">
   <input type="hidden" th:field="*{userId}" />
   <!-- User Details information -->
   <table class="table table-striped table-bordered table-hover">
    <tbody>
     <tr>
      <th class="w-25">User ID</th>
      <td th:text="*{userId}"></td>
     </tr>
     <tr>
      <th>Password</th>
      <td>
       <input type="text" class="form-control" th:field="*{password}"/>
      </td>
     </tr>
     <tr>
      <th>User Name</th>
      <td>
       <input type="text" class="form-control" th:field="*{userName}"/>
      </td>
     </tr>
     <tr>
      <th>Birthday</th>
      <td th:text="*{#dates.format(birthday, 'dd/MM/YYYY')}"></td>
```

```
      </tr>
      <tr>
        <th>Age</th>
        <td th:text="*{age}"></td>
      </tr>
      <tr>
        <th>Gender</th>
        <td th:text="*{gender == 1 ? 'Male': 'Female'}"></td>
      </tr>
      <tr>
        <th>Department name</th>
        <td>
          <span th:if="*{department != null}"
              th:text="*{department.departmentName}">
          </span>
        </td>
      </tr>
    </tbody>
  </table>
  <!-- Button area -->
  <div class="text-center">
    …(Omitted)
  </div>
  </form>
  </div>
</body>
</html>
```

Execution

Run SpringBoot to access the user details screen. The department name is displayed.

[User details screen]

8.3.3 Table join (one-to-many)

Overview

Next, you will do a one-to-many table join. The salary for each year and month is displayed on the user details screen.

[User details screen]

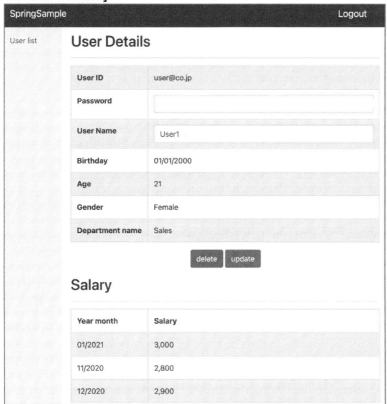

The ER diagram looks like this:

[ER diagram]

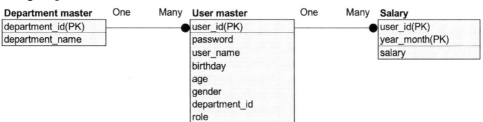

The user master and salary table have a one-to-many relationship.

Directory

The directory structure is as follows. The part where the background color is changed is the new part to be added.

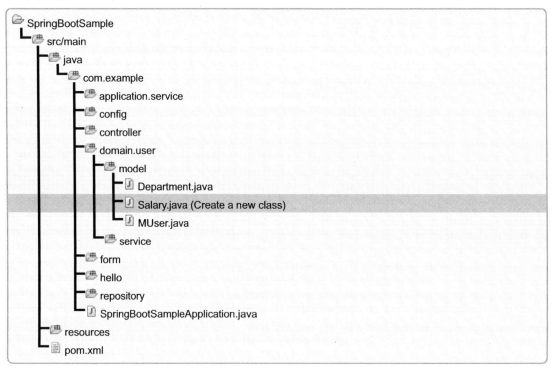

Source Code

First, modify the xml. The part where the background color is changed is the modified part.

[UserMapper.xml]

```xml
<?xml version="1.0" encoding="UTF-8"?>
<!DOCTYPE mapper PUBLIC "-//mybatis.org//DTD Mapper 3.0//EN"
 "http://mybatis.org/dtd/mybatis-3-mapper.dtd">

<!-- Mapper and xml mapping -->
<mapper namespace="com.example.repository.UserMapper">

 <!-- Mapping definition (user) -->
 <resultMap type="com.example.domain.user.model.MUser" id="user">
  <id column="user_id" property="userId" />
  <result column="password" property="password" />
  <result column="user_name" property="userName" />
  <result column="birthday" property="birthday" />
```

```xml
    <result column="age" property="age" />
    <result column="gender" property="gender" />
    <result column="department_id" property="departmentId" />
    <result column="role" property="role" />
    <association property="department" resultMap="department"/>
    <collection property="salaryList" resultMap="salary" columnPrefix="salary_"/>
</resultMap>

<!-- Mapping definition (department) -->
<resultMap type="com.example.domain.user.model.Department" id="department">
    …(Omitted)
</resultMap>

<!-- Mapping definition (salary) -->
<resultMap type="com.example.domain.user.model.Salary" id="salary">
    <id column="user_id" property="userId" />
    <id column="year_month" property="yearMonth" />
    <result column="salary" property="salary" />
</resultMap>

<!-- user registration -->
<insert id="insertOne">
    …(Omitted)
</insert>

<!-- Get user(multiple) -->
<select id="findMany" resultType="MUser">
    …(Omitted)
</select>

<!-- Get user(1record) -->
<select id="findOne" resultMap="user">
    select
        m_user.user_id
        , m_user.password
        , m_user.user_name
        , m_user.birthday
        , m_user.age
        , m_user.gender
        , m_department.department_id
        , m_department.department_name
        , t_salary.user_id as salary_user_id
        , t_salary.year_month as salary_year_month
        , t_salary.salary as salary_salary
    from
        m_user
        left join m_department
            on m_user.department_id = m_department.department_id
        left join t_salary
            on m_user.user_id = t_salary.user_id
    where
```

```
        m_user.user_id = #{userId}
</select>

<!-- Update user -->
<update id="updateOne">
    …(Omitted)
</update>

<!-- Delete user -->
<delete id="deleteOne">
    …(Omitted)
</delete>
</mapper>
```

Point 1: collection tag

The collection tag allows you to include another mapping definition in the mapping definition. Use the collection tag in a select statement that joins tables one-to-many.

Point 2: columnPrefix attribute

When joining multiple tables, the column names in the select result may be duplicated. To avoid duplicate column names, the select result may be aliased. However, if an alias is given, it will no longer match the column name in the mapping definition. The columnPrefix attribute is used to solve the problem.

Let's check how to use the columnPrefix attribute in the sample code.

[UserMapper.xml]

```
<!-- Mapping definition (user) -->
<resultMap type="com.example.domain.user.model.MUser" id="user">
  …(Omitted)
  <collection property="salaryList" resultMap="salary" columnPrefix="salary_"/>
</resultMap>

  …(Omitted)

<!-- Mapping definition (salary) -->
<resultMap type="com.example.domain.user.model.Salary" id="salary">
  <id column="user_id" property="userId" />
  <id column="year_month" property="yearMonth" />
  <result column="salary" property="salary" />
</resultMap>

  …(Omitted)

<select id="findOne" resultMap="user">
    select
```

```
      m_user.user_id
    , m_user.password
    , m_user.user_name
    , m_user.birthday
    , m_user.age
    , m_user.gender
    , m_department.department_id
    , m_department.department_name
    , t_salary.user_id as salary_user_id
    , t_salary.year_month as salary_year_month
    , t_salary.salary as salary_salary
  from
    m_user
    left join m_department
      on m_user.department_id = m_department.department_id
    left join t_salary
      on m_user.user_id = t_salary.user_id
  where
    m_user.user_id = #{userId}
</select>
```

As a result of the select statement, "salary_" is added to the beginning of the alias. Set this to the value of the columnPrefix attribute. This will allow the column prefixed with the string "salary_" to match the salary table mapping definition.

By the way, you can also add the columnPrefix attribute to the association tag.

Next, create an entity class for the Salary table.
[Salary.java]

```
package com.example.domain.user.model;

import lombok.Data;

@Data
public class Salary {
    private String userId;
    private String yearMonth;
    private Integer salary;
}
```

Then add the salary entity list to the user entity class. The part where the background color is changed is the modified part.
[MUser.java]

```
@Data
public class MUser {
    private String userId;
```

```
    private String password;
    private String userName;
    private Date birthday;
    private Integer age;
    private Integer gender;
    private Integer departmentId;
    private String role;
    private Department department;
    private List<Salary> salaryList;
}
```

Also add the salary entity list to the form class on the user details screen. The part where the background color is changed is the modified part.

[UserDetailForm.java]

```
@Data
public class UserDetailForm {
    private String userId;
    private String password;
    private String userName;
    private Date birthday;
    private Integer age;
    private Integer gender;
    private Department department;
    private List<Salary> salaryList;
}
```

Then modify the controller on the user details screen. The part where the background color is changed is the modified part.

[UserDetailController.java]

```
@Controller
@RequestMapping("/user")
public class UserDetailController {

    @Autowired
    private UserService userService;

    @Autowired
    private ModelMapper modelMapper;

    /** Display user details screen */
    @GetMapping("/detail/{userId:.+}")
    public String getUser(UserDetailForm form, Model model,
            @PathVariable("userId") String userId) {

        // Get user
        MUser user = userService.getUserOne(userId);
        user.setPassword(null);
```

```
    // Convert MUser to form
    form = modelMapper.map(user, UserDetailForm.class);
    form.setSalaryList(user.getSalaryList());

    // Registered in Model
    model.addAttribute("userDetailForm", form);

    // Display user details screen
    return "user/detail";
  }

  /** User update process */
  @PostMapping(value = "/detail", params = "update")
  public String updateUser(UserDetailForm form, Model model) {
    ...(Omitted)
  }

  /** User delete process */
  @PostMapping(value = "/detail", params = "delete")
  public String deleteUser(UserDetailForm form, Model model) {
    ...(Omitted)
  }
}
```

Since ModelMapper cannot copy List, call setter.

Finally, modify the user details screen. The part where the background color is changed is the modified part.

[detail.html]

```
<!DOCTYPE html>
<html xmlns:th="http://www.thymeleaf.org"
  xmlns:layout="http://www.ultraq.net.nz/thymeleaf/layout"
  layout:decorate="~{layout/layout}">
<head>
  <title>User Details</title>
  <!-- Read CSS -->
  <link rel="stylesheet" th:href="@{/css/user/list.css}">
</head>
<body>
  <div layout:fragment="content">
    <div class="header border-bottom">
      <h1 class="h2">User Details</h1>
    </div>
    <form id="user-detail-form" method="post" th:action="@{/user/detail}"
      class="form-signup" th:object="${userDetailForm}">
      <input type="hidden" th:field="*{userId}" />
      <!-- User Details information -->
      <table class="table table-striped table-bordered table-hover">
        ...(Omitted)
```

```
    </table>
    <!-- Button area -->
    <div class="text-center">
      ...(Omitted)
    </div>
    <!-- Salary information -->
    <th:block th:if="*{salaryList != null and salaryList.size() > 0}">
      <div class="header border-bottom">
        <h1 class="h2">Salary</h1>
      </div>
      <table class="table table-striped table-bordered table-hover">
        <thead>
          <tr>
            <th class="w-25">Year month</th>
            <th>Salary</th>
          </tr>
        </thead>
        <tbody>
          <tr th:each="item: *{salaryList}">
            <td th:text="${item.yearMonth}"></td>
            <td th:text="${#numbers.formatInteger(item.salary, 3, 'COMMA')}">
            </td>
          </tr>
        </tbody>
      </table>
    </th:block>
  </form>
 </div>
</body>
</html>
```

Point: "th:block"

You may not want to add HTML tags when the result of the "th:if" attribute returns true. For example, the div tag remains in the following code:

[Example: "th:if" returns true]

```
<div th:if="${Some conditional expression}">
 <p>Sample</p>
</div>
```

[Generated HTML]

```
<div>
 <p>Sample</p>
</div>
```

If you use "th:block", the tag itself of "th:block" disappears. And only the code inside the "th:block" tag remains.

[Example: "th:block"]

```
<th:block th:if="${Some conditional expression}">
  <p>Sample</p>
</th:block>
```

[Generated HTML]

```
<p>Sample</p>
```

Execution

Run SpringBoot and access the User Details screen for "user1".

[User details screen] (user1)

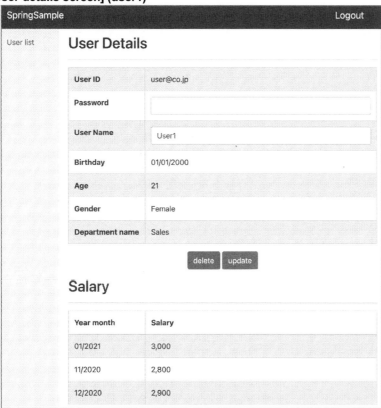

The salary for each year and month is displayed.

8.4 Transaction

Here you will learn about Spring transactions. Not only MyBatis, but also when using JDBC or JPA in Spring, manage transactions with the same code.

- Type of transaction
- Implementation of transactions
- Configuring declarative transactions

8.4.1 Type of transaction

Begin by learning about the type of transaction. There are two types of Spring transactions:

- Explicit transaction
- Declarative transaction

An explicit transaction is a direct way of writing code for a transaction.

A declarative transaction is a way to implement a transaction simply by annotating it. You can eliminate non-essential code by just annotating it. As a result, you rarely use explicit transactions.

8.4.2 Implementation of transactions

Overview

Raise an intentional exception during user update processing. It then checks to see if it was rolled back.

Directory

There is no change in the directory structure.

Source Code

Modify the user service implementation class. The part where the background color is changed is the modified part.
[UserServiceImpl.java]

```
package com.example.domain.user.service.impl;

import java.util.List;

import org.springframework.beans.factory.annotation.Autowired;
```

```java
import org.springframework.stereotype.Service;
import org.springframework.transaction.annotation.Transactional;

import com.example.domain.user.model.MUser;
import com.example.domain.user.service.UserService;
import com.example.repository.UserMapper;

@Service
public class UserServiceImpl implements UserService {

    @Autowired
    private UserMapper mapper;

    /** User signup */
    @Override
    public void signup(MUser user) {
        ...(Omitted)
    }

    /** Get user */
    @Override
    public List<MUser> getUsers(MUser user) {
        return mapper.findMany(user);
    }

    /** Get user(1record) */
    @Override
    public MUser getUserOne(String userId) {
        return mapper.findOne(userId);
    }

    /** Update user */
    @Transactional
    @Override
    public void updateUserOne(String userId,
            String password,
            String userName) {
        mapper.updateOne(userId, password, userName);

        // Raise an exception
        int i = 1 / 0;
    }

    /** Delete user */
    @Override
    public void deleteUserOne(String userId) {
        int count = mapper.deleteOne(userId);
    }
}
```

Point: @Transactional

You can implement a transaction by annotating the method with @Transactional. If an exception occurs within a method with this annotation, it will be automatically rolled back.

This annotation can also be attached to classes as well as methods. If you annotate a class, all methods implement the transaction.

Then modify the controller on the user details screen. The part where the background color is changed is the modified part.

[UserDetailController.java]

```java
@Controller
@RequestMapping("/user")
@Slf4j
public class UserDetailController {

    @Autowired
    private UserService userService;

    @Autowired
    private ModelMapper modelMapper;

    /** Display user details screen */
    @GetMapping("/detail/{userId:.+}")
    public String getUser(UserDetailForm form, Model model,
            @PathVariable("userId") String userId) {
        ...(Omitted)
    }

    /** User update process */
    @PostMapping(value = "/detail", params = "update")
    public String updateUser(UserDetailForm form, Model model) {

        try {
            // Update user
            userService.updateUserOne(form.getUserId(),
                    form.getPassword(),
                    form.getUserName());
        } catch (Exception e) {
            log.error("Error in user update", e);
        }

        // Redirect to user list screen
        return "redirect:/user/list";
    }

    /** User delete process */
    @PostMapping(value = "/detail", params = "delete")
```

```
public String deleteUser(UserDetailForm form, Model model) {
    …(Omitted)
  }
}
```

Note: Stack trace output

To check the details of the error content, a stack trace is output when an error occurs. If you pass the Exception class to Lombok's log method, it will output a stack trace.

Execution

Run SpringBoot and access the user details screen. Change the user name and press the "update" button.

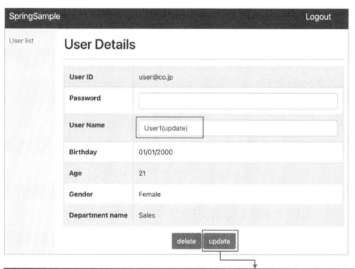

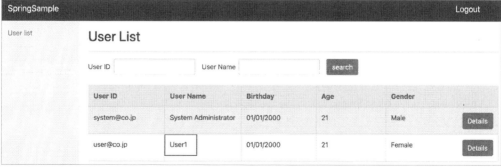

The user name has not been changed. The following error log is output.

[Log] (Excerpt)

```
==>  Preparing: update m_user set password = ? , user_name = ? where user_id = ?
==> Parameters: password(String), User1(update)(String), user@co.jp(String)
<==   Updates: 1
Error in user update

java.lang.ArithmeticException: / by zero
…(Omitted)
```

If an error occurred, it was confirmed that it was rolled back.

Finally, comment out the code that deliberately caused the exception.

[UserServiceImpl.java] (Excerpt)

```
// Raise an exception
// int i = 1 / 0;
```

8.4.3 Configuring declarative transactions

Here you will learn about setting up declarative transactions.

To configure a transaction, set the @Transactional annotation with the following attributes and values:

[List of Transaction Settings]

Attribute	Description
value	When using multiple transaction managers, specify the "Qualifier" of the transaction manager to be used. Optional if you want to use the default transaction manager.
transactionManager	Alias for value
propagation	Specifies the propagation level of the transaction. Details will be explained later.
isolation	Specifies the isolation level for the transaction. Details will be explained later.
timeout	Specifies the timeout period (in seconds) for the transaction. The default is -1.

	However, the default value depends on the specifications and settings of the database being used.
readOnly	Specifies the read-only flag for the transaction. The default is false (not read-only).
rollbackFor	Specifies a list of exception classes for which to roll back a transaction. RuntimeException is subject to rollback by default.
rollbackForClassName	Specifies a list of exception class names for which transactions are to be rolled back. By default, nothing is specified.
noRollbackFor	Specifies a list of exception classes to exclude from transaction rollback. By default, nothing is specified.
noRollbackForClassName	Specifies a list of exception class names to exclude from transaction rollback. By default, nothing is specified.

The isolation and propagation levels are important for setting up transactions.

What is transaction independence?

First, the isolation level is explained. But, in order to understand the isolation level, I explain the transaction independence.

If many users use the application, there are multiple transactions. If multiple transactions reference and update different data, nothing is wrong. However, care must be taken when referring to the same data. Some common examples of transaction problems include the following:

[Example: Transaction independence]

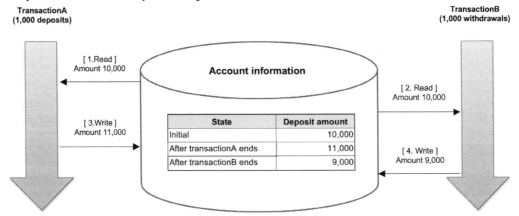

1. First, transaction A reads the bank account information.
2. Transaction B then reads the bank account information.
3. Transaction A has updated to 11,000 to increase the amount in the account by +1,000.
4. Transaction B has updated to 9,000 to reduce the amount in the account by -1,000.

The amount in the account was 1,000 deposited and 1,000 withdrawn. However, the amount is now 9,000. In such cases, transaction B should wait for transaction A to finish.

In this way, even if multiple transactions are executed at the same time, normal processing must be performed. This is called transaction independence (or isolation).

The isolation level specifies this level of independence. For the isolation level, specify the following values for the isolation attribute. However, note that some levels may not be available depending on the database product you are using.

[Transaction isolation level]

Isolation level	Description
DEFAULT	Use the default isolation level of database.
READ_UNCOMMITTED	Reads data that no other transaction has committed. If it is rolled back, invalid data is searched.
READ_COMMITTED	Data that has not been committed by another transaction cannot be read.
REPEATABLE_READ	If data is read multiple times within a transaction, The same value is read even if other transactions change the data in the middle.

SERIALIZABLE	Process transactions one by one, and so on.

[Typical issues in independence]

The following is a brief explanation of some of the typical issues with independence. There are three problems:

- Dirty read
- Non-repeatable read
- Phantom read

- **Dirty read**

  Reading the data before committing.

- **Non-repeatable read**

  Read the same data many times in a transaction. In the meantime, another transaction updates the data. In that case, the data to be read will change from the middle.

- **Phantom read**

  Read the same data many times in a transaction. In the meantime, another transaction adds new data. If this happens, the number of records to be processed will increase in the middle of the transaction.

The isolation levels introduced earlier and the correspondence table for these issues are as follows.

[Isolation level]

Isolation level	Dirty read	Non-repeatable read	Phantom read
READ_UNCOMMITTED	NG	NG	NG
READ_COMMITTED	OK	NG	NG
REPEATABLE_READ	OK	OK	NG
SERIALIZABLE	OK	OK	OK

(OK: Prevent, NG: Do not prevent)

Make sure you set the appropriate isolation level.

What is transaction propagation level?

Next, I will explain the propagation level. The propagation level determines whether or not a new transaction is created and started.

Especially important is when a service calls another service. You can configure whether to start a transaction, join an existing transaction, and so on.

[Propagation level]

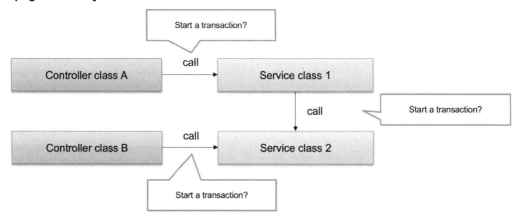

You can set the propagation level to:

[Propagation level]

Propagation level	Description
REQUIRED	If no transaction exists, REQUIRED starts a new transaction. Default propagation level. If a transaction already exists, it is used.
REQUIRES_NEW	A new transaction is always created.
MANDATORY	MANDATORY assumes that a transaction already exists. If a transaction already exists, it is used. If no transaction exists, an exception is raised.
NEVER	If "NEVER" is specified, no transaction is used. If a transaction already exists, an exception is raised.

NOT_SUPPORTED	NOT_SUPPORTED does not use transactions. If a transaction already exists, the transaction is suspended. Executes processing without using transactions while the system is paused. When processing is complete, restart the stopped transaction.
SUPPORTS	If the transaction does not exist, it will not be created. If a transaction already exists, it is used.
NESTED	Creates a nested transaction. If no transaction exists, a new transaction is started. If a transaction already exists, it is used. In that case, it is treated as if it were a nested transaction.

Please check the table below as it may be difficult to understand if it is just an explanation.

[Behavior by propagation level]

Propagation level	Set the propagation level for service2	
	Call service 2 directly	Call service 2 via service 1
REQUIRED	Transaction start	Join service1 transaction
REQUIRES_NEW	Transaction start	Transaction start
MANDATORY	Throw an exception	Join service1 transaction
NEVER	It does not perform the transaction	Throw an exception
NOT_SUPPORTED	It does not perform the transaction	It does not perform the transaction
SUPPORTS	It does not perform the transaction	Join service1 transaction
NESTED	Transaction start	Partial transaction start

This completes the learning of transactions.

Summary

Here's what you've learned in this chapter:

[Basic]

- To use MyBatis, annotate the Java interface with @Mapper.
- Use the namespace attribute of the mapper tag to map the Java interface to an xml file.
- Map methods and SQL using id attributes such as insert tags.
- To embed method arguments in SQL, specify #{parameter name}.
- Use the resultType and resultMap attributes to return a select result.
- The resultMap attribute can be used to make O/R mappings for different cases.
- The @Param annotation allows you to specify the name of the parameter to embed in SQL.

[Advanced]

- Dynamic SQL can be generated with the if tag.
- You can use the where tag to generate SQL that does not require a where clause.
- Use the association tag for one-to-one table joins.
- Use the collection tag for one-to-many table joins.

[Transaction]

- To implement a transaction, use the @Transactional annotation.
- Attributes of @Transactional can be used to set isolation and propagation levels.

9. AOP

In this chapter you will learn about AOP.

- Overview of AOP
- AOP implementation

9.1 Overview of AOP

First, I will explain the outline of AOP.

- What is AOP?
- AOP terminology
- How AOP Works

9.1.1 What is AOP?

AOP is to extract common processes and manage them collectively. AOP stands for Aspect Oriented Programming.

With AOP, you can put non-essential code in one place. You can then decide which class or method to apply the code to.

For example, suppose you want to log the start and end of all controller methods. If you don't use AOP, you would write code like this:

[Sample Code Without AOP]

```
@Controller
@Slf4j
public class SampleController {

  @GetMapping("/sample")
  public String get() {
    log.info("Method start: SampleController get");

    ...(Some processing)

    log.info("Method end: SampleController get");
  }
}
```

This is a very bad code. This is because there are three problems:

- The readability of the code is reduced.
- Processing may be forgotten.
- If there is a change in the log output content, the number of corrections will be enormous.

If you implement the above code with AOP, it will be as follows.

[AOP Sample Code]

```
@Aspect
@Component
@Slf4j
public class LogAspect {

    @Before("@within(org.springframework.stereotype.Controller)")
    public void startLog(JoinPoint jp) {
        log.info("Method start: " + jp.getSignature());
    }

    @After("@within(org.springframework.stereotype.Controller)")
    public void endLog(JoinPoint jp) {
        log.info("Method end: " + jp.getSignature());
    }
}
```

With this alone, the log will be output before and after the execution of all controllers. It also eliminates the need for log output code on the controller. You can change the output to the log by modifying only the AOP code.

9.1.2 AOP terminology

AOP has terminology. If you don't know the terminology first, you won't be able to understand it. AOP terminology is as follows:

[AOP terminology]

Terminology	Description
Advice	It is the processing content to be executed in AOP.
Pointcut	It is the target (class or method) that executes the process.
JoinPoint	It is the timing to execute the process.

Next, the JoinPoint (execution timing) is divided into the following five types.

[JoinPoint type]

Execution timing	Description
Before	Executes the process before the target method is executed.
After	Executes the process after the target method is executed.
AfterReturning	The process is executed only when the target method ends normally.
Around	Execute the process before and after executing the target method.
AfterThrowing	The process is executed only when the target method terminates abnormally.

The figure below shows these Join Points (execution timing).

[Before]

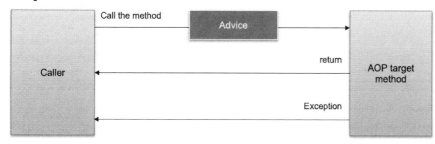

[After]

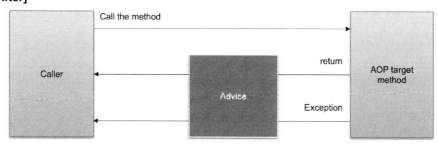

[AfterReturning]

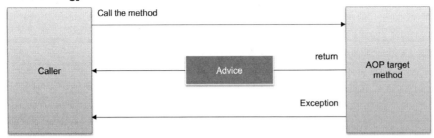

[Around]

[AfterThrowing]

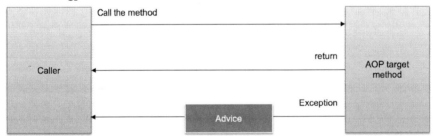

9.1.3 How AOP Works

I will explain how AOP internally works. Understanding this makes it easier to understand AOP.

The mechanism of AOP is as follows.

[How AOP works]

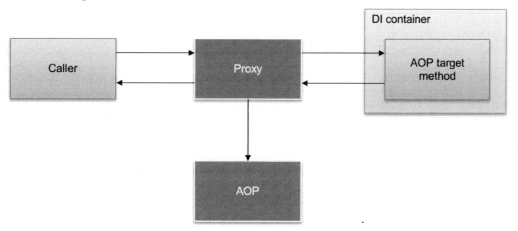

First, Spring tries to call the method of the bean registered in the DI container. A bean is a class with annotations such as @Controller and @Service.

Call the method of the service from the controller as follows:
[Sample code]

```
@Controller
public SampleController {

    @Autowired
    private SampleService service;

    public void method() {
        service.someMethod();
    }
}
```

If you really call someMethod() directly, you can't put AOP processing before or after the method.

So Spring calls the bean's method via Proxy. The Proxy then calls the AOP process and the Bean method.

Because we are using DI, we can use AOP for common processing. This is the internal mechanism of AOP.

9.2 AOP implementation

After understanding AOP, you will implement it.

- How to specify Pointcut
- Before/After implementation
- Around implementation

9.2.1 How to specify Pointcut

Before starting implementation with AOP, let's learn how to specify Pointcut (execution target). There are four ways to specify it.

[How to specify Pointcut (execution target)]

Pointcut	Description
execution	Specify any class or method using a regular expression.
bean	Specifies the bean name registered in the DI container.
@annotation	Specify the execution target using the annotation name including the package name. The method with the specified annotation is the target.
@within	Specify the annotation name including the package name. All methods of the class with the specified annotation are subject to AOP.

9.2.2 Before/After implementation

Overview

Outputs a start and end log each time a method of the UserService is executed.

Implement AOP so that the following log is output when the user list screen is displayed.

[Log] (Excerpt)

```
Method start: List com.example.domain.user.service.impl.UserServiceImpl.getUsers(MUser)
Method end: List com.example.domain.user.service.impl.UserServiceImpl.getUsers(MUser)
```

Directory

The directory structure is as follows. The part where the background color is changed is the new part to be added.

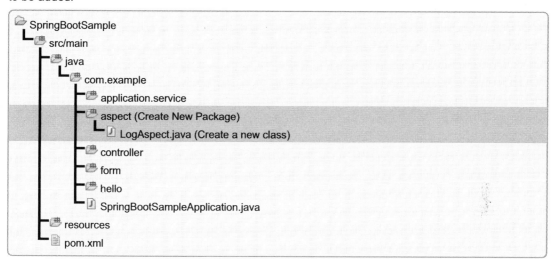

Source Code

A library is required to use AOP. Therefore, add the following code in the dependencies tag of pom.xml. The part where the background color is changed is the added part.

[pom.xml]

```xml
<dependencies>
...
<!-- Spring AOP -->
<dependency>
  <groupId>org.springframework</groupId>
  <artifactId>spring-aop</artifactId>
</dependency>
<!-- AspectJ -->
<dependency>
  <groupId>org.aspectj</groupId>
  <artifactId>aspectjweaver</artifactId>
</dependency>
...
</dependencies>
```

Implement AOP.

[LogAspect.java]

```java
package com.example.aspect;
```

```java
import org.aspectj.lang.JoinPoint;
import org.aspectj.lang.annotation.After;
import org.aspectj.lang.annotation.Aspect;
import org.aspectj.lang.annotation.Before;
import org.springframework.stereotype.Component;

import lombok.extern.slf4j.Slf4j;

@Aspect
@Component
@Slf4j
public class LogAspect {

  /**
   * Log output before executing the service.
   * Target: [UserService] is included in the class name.
   */
  @Before("execution(* *..*.*UserService.*(..))")
  public void startLog(JoinPoint jp) {
     log.info("Method start: " + jp.getSignature());
  }

  /**
   * Log output after executing the service.
   * Target: [UserService] is included in the class name.
   */
  @After("execution(* *..*.*UserService.*(..))")
  public void endLog(JoinPoint jp) {
     log.info("Method end: " + jp.getSignature());
  }
}
```

Point 1: AOP Class

Annotate AOP classes with @Aspect and @Component.

Point 2: JoinPoint (execution timing)

To specify a JoinPoint, annotate the method with the same name as the JoinPoint. That is, annotate the method with:

[JoinPoint annotations]

- @Before
- @After
- @AfterReturning
- @Around

- @AfterThrowing

Point 3: execution

To specify which classes or methods are subject to AOP, specify a Pointcut within an annotation such as @Before. In the sample code, "execution" is used to specify Pointcut (execution target). The syntax of "execution" is as follows.

[execution syntax]

```
execution(return-value package-name.class-name.method-name(argument))
```

Regular expressions can be used for package names, class names, and so on.

[How to use regular expressions]

- *** (asterisk)**
  Use the asterisk to represent any string. In the package part, an asterisk represents a single package name. In the argument part of the method, an asterisk represents one argument.

- **.. (2 dots)**
  Two consecutive dots represent any value greater than or equal to zero. In the package part, two dots represent a package with zero or more characters. In the argument part of the method, two dots represent zero or more arguments.

- **+ (plus)**
  If you specify a plus after the class name, subclasses of the specified class are included.

Execution

Run Spring Boot and access the following URL.

[URL]
http://localhost:8080/user/list

The following log should be output.
[Log] (Excerpt)

```
Method start: List com.example.domain.user.service.impl.UserServiceImpl.getUsers(MUser)
Method end: List com.example.domain.user.service.impl.UserServiceImpl.getUsers(MUser)
```

※The MyBatis log is omitted.

205

9.2.3 Around implementation

Overview

Implement AOP to output start and end logs for all controller methods.

Directory

There is no change in the directory structure.

Source Code

Add a method for AOP. The part where the background color is changed is the modified part.

[LogAspect.java]

```java
package com.example.aspect;

import org.aspectj.lang.JoinPoint;
import org.aspectj.lang.ProceedingJoinPoint;
import org.aspectj.lang.annotation.After;
import org.aspectj.lang.annotation.Around;
import org.aspectj.lang.annotation.Aspect;
import org.aspectj.lang.annotation.Before;
import org.springframework.stereotype.Component;

import lombok.extern.slf4j.Slf4j;

@Aspect
@Component
@Slf4j
public class LogAspect {

    /**
     * Log output before executing the service.
     * Target: [UserService] is included in the class name.
     */
    @Before("execution(* *..*.*UserService.*(..))")
    public void startLog(JoinPoint jp) {
        log.info("Method start: " + jp.getSignature());
    }

    /**
     * Log output after executing the service.
     * Target: [UserService] is included in the class name.
     */
    @After("execution(* *..*.*UserService.*(..))")
```

```java
public void endLog(JoinPoint jp) {
    log.info("Method end: " + jp.getSignature());
}

/** Log output before and after the controller is executed */
//@Around("bean(*Controller)")
//@Around("@annotation(org.springframework.web.bind.annotation.GetMapping)")
@Around("@within(org.springframework.stereotype.Controller)")
public Object startLog(ProceedingJoinPoint jp) throws Throwable {

    // Output start log
    log.info("Method start: " + jp.getSignature());

    try {
        // Method execution
        Object result = jp.proceed();

        // Output end log
        log.info("Method end: " + jp.getSignature());

        // Return the execution result to the caller
        return result;

    } catch (Exception e) {
        // Output error log
        log.error("Method abend: " + jp.getSignature());

        // Rethrow the error
        throw e;
    }
}
}
```

Point 1: @Around

By adding the @Around annotation to the method, you can insert processing before and after the AOP execution target. The mechanism is that it directly calls the method to be executed by AOP. In the above sample code, the method to be executed by AOP is called in the following part.

[LogAspect.java]

```java
// Method execution
Object result = jp.proceed();
...
// Return the execution result to the caller
return result;
```

Please note that if you do not include the above processing, the method will not execute normally.

Point 2: bean

If you use "bean" as the Pointcut (execution target), you can specify the target of AOP by the bean name registered in the DI container. Of course, regular expressions can also be used.

[How to specify bean]

```
bean(Bean-name)
```

Although commented out in the sample code, classes with Controller at the end of the bean name are subject to AOP.

Point 3: @annotation

If you use "@annotation" for Pointcut (execution target), the method with the specified annotation will be the target of AOP. Include the package name in the annotation name. Although commented out in the sample code, methods with @GetMapping are subject to AOP.

Point 4: @within

If you use @within, all methods of the class with the specified annotation will be the target of AOP. Include the package name in the annotation name.

In the sample code, all methods of the class annotated with @Controller are targeted for AOP.

Execution

Run Spring Boot and access the following URL.

[URL]
http://localhost:8080/login

The following log should be output.
[Log] (Excerpt)

```
Method start: String com.example.controller.LoginController.getLogin()
Method end: String com.example.controller.LoginController.getLogin()
```

※The MyBatis log is omitted.

Summary

Here's what you've learned in this chapter:

[AOP Overview]

- AOP is a mechanism for collectively managing common processing.

[AOP terminology]

- Advice: Processing content
- Pointcut: Execution target
- JoinPoint: Execution timing

[How to specify JoinPoint (execution timing)]

- Annotate the following JoinPoint (execution timing) to the method of AOP class.

    1. Before: Before execution
    2. After: After execution (normal termination/abnormal termination)
    3. Around: Before and after execution
    4. AfterReturning: After normal completion
    5. AfterThrowing: After abnormal termination

[How to specify Pointcut (execution target)]

- Specify the following Pointcut (execution target) in the annotation of JoinPoint (execution timing).

    1. execution(return-value package-name.class-name.method-name(argument))
    2. bean(Bean-name)
    3. @annotation(package-name.annotation-name)
    4. @within(package-name.annotation-name)

[How to implement AOP]

- Annotate AOP classes with @Aspect and @Component.
- Annotate JoinPoint (execution timing) to methods of AOP class.
- Specify Pointcut (execution target) in the annotation of JoinPoint.

10. Error Handling

In this chapter you will learn about error handling. Here's what you'll learn in this chapter:

- Creating an Error Screen
- How to Implement Exception Handling

10.1 Creating an Error Screen

The first step is to create an error screen. There are two types of error screens:

- Common error screen
- Error screen for each HTTP error

10.1.1 Common error screen

Overview

There are some bugs in the applications you have created. For example, if you try to register a user ID that has already been registered, an error will occur. Then, the following error screen will be displayed.

[Whitelabel error page]

Whitelabel Error Page

This application has no explicit mapping for /error, so you are seeing this as a fallback.

Wed Apr 28 15:14:02 JST 2021
There was an unexpected error (type=Internal Server Error, status=500).
Error updating database. Cause: org.h2.jdbc.JdbcSQLIntegrityConstraintViolationException:

This is a WhiteLabel error page provided by Spring. However, there are still two problems:

- There is a security problem because the error details are displayed.
- When an error occurs, the user does not know what to do.

Therefore, create a common error screen that allows you to jump to the login page.

[Common Error Screen]

500 Internal Server Error

Error updating database. Cause: org.h2.jdbc.JdbcSQLI
VALUES 1" Unique index or primary key violation: "PUBLIC.
gender , department_id , role) values (? , ? , ? , ? , ? , ? , ?
理/10-1-1.共通エラーページ/SpringBootSample10-1-1/targe
SQL: insert into m_user(user_id , password , user_name , b
org.h2.jdbc.JdbcSQLIntegrityConstraintViolationException:
violation: "PUBLIC.PRIMARY_KEY_8 ON PUBLIC.M_USER(U:
, ? , ? , ? , ? , ? , ? , ?) [23505-200] ; ユニークインデックス、
"PUBLIC.PRIMARY_KEY_8 ON PUBLIC.M_USER(USER_ID) V
, ? , ? , ? , ?) [23505-200]; nested exception is org.h2.jdbc.
PUBLIC.M_USER(USER_ID) VALUES 1" Unique index or prir
user_name , birthday , age , gender , department_id , role)

Please return to the login screen

| Return to login screen |

Directory

The directory structure is as follows. The part where the background color is changed is the new part to be added.

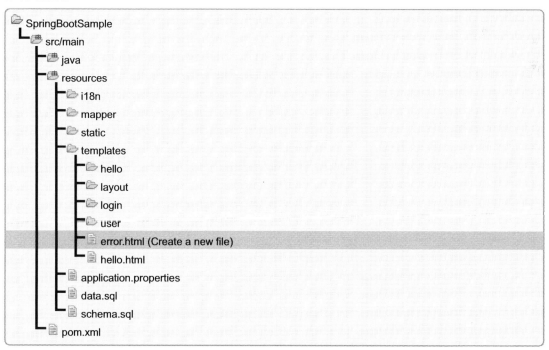

Point: Common error screen

Creating a common error screen is very easy. Because it just creates a file called "error.html" under "src/main/resources/templates".

Source Code

Creates a common error screen.

[error.html]

```
<!DOCTYPE html>
<html xmlns:th="http://www.thymeleaf.org">
<head>
  <meta charset="utf-8" />
  <title>Error</title>
</head>
<body>
  <h1 th:text="${status} + ' ' + ${error}"></h1>
  <p th:text="${message}"></p>
  <p>Please return to the login screen</p>
  <form method="post" th:action="@{/logout}">
    <button class="btn btn-link" type="submit">Return to login screen</button>
  </form>
</body>
</html>
```

Point: Display of various error contents

You can get the details of the error contents by specifying the following key. Spring will set these values automatically.

Code	Description
${status}	Contains the HTTP error code.
${error}	Displays a summary of HTTP errors.
${message}	An error message is displayed.

Execution

Run SpringBoot to access the user signup screen.

Enter "system@co.jp" in the User ID field to register the user. A unique constraint violation occurs because the user ID is registered in the initial data. Therefore, the screen moves to the common error screen.

[User signup screen]

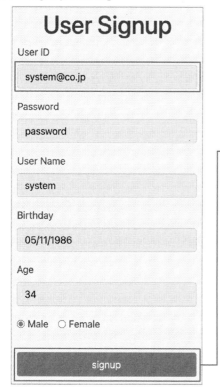

500 Internal Server Error

Error updating database. Cause: org.h2.jdbc.JdbcSQL
VALUES 1" Unique index or primary key violation: "PUBLIC
gender , department_id , role) values (? , ? , ? , ? , ? , ? , ?
理/10-1-1.共通エラーページ/SpringBootSample10-1-1/targe
SQL: insert into m_user(user_id , password , user_name , I
org.h2.jdbc.JdbcSQLIntegrityConstraintViolationException:
violation: "PUBLIC.PRIMARY_KEY_8 ON PUBLIC.M_USER(U
, ? , ? , ? , ? , ? , ? , ?) [23505-200] ; ユニークインデックス、
"PUBLIC.PRIMARY_KEY_8 ON PUBLIC.M_USER(USER_ID) \
, ? , ? , ? , ?) [23505-200]; nested exception is org.h2.jdbc
PUBLIC.M_USER(USER_ID) VALUES 1" Unique index or pri
user_name , birthday , age , gender , department_id , role)

Please return to the login screen

Return to login screen

213

10.1.2 Error screen for each HTTP error

Overview

Using Spring's default function, you can also prepare an error screen for each HTTP error. Create a screen for 404 errors. A 404 error is an error when an HTTP request is sent to a URL that does not exist.

[404 Error Screen]

404 Not Found

This is a 404 error page

Return to login screen

Directory

The directory structure is as follows. The part where the background color is changed is the new part to be added.

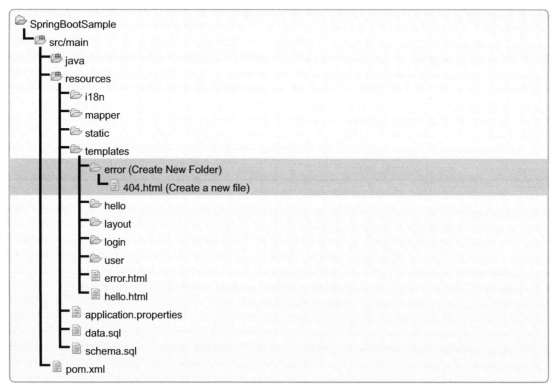

Point: Error screen for each HTTP error

It is very easy to create a screen for each HTTP error. Simply prepare the file under "src/main/resources/templates/error". The file name must be the same as the HTTP error code. To create a screen that responds to 404 errors, prepare a file called "404.html".

Source Code

Creates a 404 error screen.
[404.html]

```
<!DOCTYPE html>
<html xmlns:th="http://www.thymeleaf.org">
<head>
 <meta charset="utf-8" />
 <title>404Error</title>
</head>
<body>
 <h1 th:text="${status} + ' ' + ${error}"></h1>
 <p>This is a 404 error page</p>
 <form method="post" th:action="@{/logout}">
  <button class="btn btn-link" type="submit">Return to login screen</button>
 </form>
</body>
</html>
```

Execution

Run SpringBoot and access a non-existent URL. For example, go to "http://localhost:8080/hoge". A 404 error occurs and the following screen is displayed.

[404 Error screen]

404 Not Found

This is a 404 error page

Return to login screen

10.2 How to Implement Exception Handling

Next, you will implement exception handling in Spring.

Spring provides several mechanisms that allow exception handling to be standardized. It allows developers to focus on implementing essential processing. There are three ways to implement exception handling in Spring:

- Exception Handling in the @AfterThrowing Aspect
- Exception handling for each controller class
- exception handling for the entire web application

10.2.1 Exception Handling in the @AfterThrowing Aspect

Overview

The @AfterThrowing aspect is used to output a log when an error occurs. If a DataAccessException occurs, modify the application to output the following log.

[Log] (Excerpt)

DataAccessException has occurred

Directory

The directory structure is as follows. The part where the background color is changed is the new part to be added.

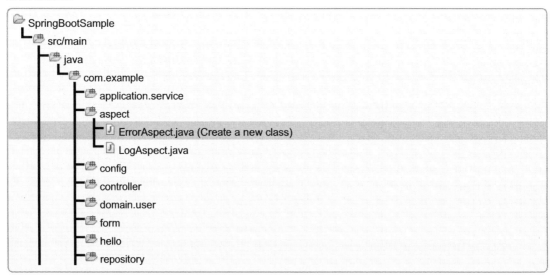

```
└ 🗋 SpringBootSampleApplication.java
├ 📁 resources
└ 📄 pom.xml
```

Source Code

Create an AOP that outputs a log when an error occurs.

[ErrorAspect.java]

```java
package com.example.aspect;

import org.aspectj.lang.annotation.AfterThrowing;
import org.aspectj.lang.annotation.Aspect;
import org.springframework.dao.DataAccessException;
import org.springframework.stereotype.Component;

import lombok.extern.slf4j.Slf4j;

@Aspect
@Component
@Slf4j
public class ErrorAspect {

    @AfterThrowing(value = "execution(* *..*..*(..)) &&"
        + "(bean(*Controller) || bean(*Service) || bean(*Repository))",
        throwing = "ex")
    public void throwingNull(DataAccessException ex) {
        // Exception handling (log output)
        log.error("DataAccessException has occurred");
    }
}
```

Point: @AfterThrowing

By annotating @AfterThrowing, you can implement AOP when an exception occurs. In the throwing attribute, specify the method argument of the exception class.

Execution

Run SpringBoot to access the user signup screen.

Enter "system@co.jp" in the User ID field to register the user. A unique constraint violation occurs.

The following log will be output.

[Log] (Excerpt)

DataAccessException has occurred

10.2.2 Exception handling for each controller class

Overview

In this section, you will learn about exception handling when an unexpected exception occurs in a controller class.

When an error occurs on the user signup screen, the following message is displayed on the common error screen.

[Common error screen]

```
500 INTERNAL_SERVER_ERROR

An exception occurred in SignupController

Please return to the login screen

[ Return to login screen ]
```

Directory

There is no change in the directory structure.

Source Code

Modify the controller on the user signup screen. The part where the background color is changed is the modified part.

[SignupController.java]

```java
package com.example.controller;

import java.util.Locale;
import java.util.Map;

import org.modelmapper.ModelMapper;
import org.springframework.beans.factory.annotation.Autowired;
import org.springframework.dao.DataAccessException;
import org.springframework.http.HttpStatus;
import org.springframework.stereotype.Controller;
import org.springframework.ui.Model;
import org.springframework.validation.BindingResult;
import org.springframework.validation.annotation.Validated;
import org.springframework.web.bind.annotation.ExceptionHandler;
import org.springframework.web.bind.annotation.GetMapping;
```

```java
import org.springframework.web.bind.annotation.ModelAttribute;
import org.springframework.web.bind.annotation.PostMapping;
import org.springframework.web.bind.annotation.RequestMapping;

import com.example.application.service.UserApplicationService;
import com.example.domain.user.model.MUser;
import com.example.domain.user.service.UserService;
import com.example.form.GroupOrder;
import com.example.form.SignupForm;

import lombok.extern.slf4j.Slf4j;

@Controller
@RequestMapping("/user")
@Slf4j
public class SignupController {

    @Autowired
    private UserApplicationService userApplicationService;

    @Autowired
    private UserService userService;

    @Autowired
    private ModelMapper modelMapper;

    /** Display the user signup screen */
    @GetMapping("/signup")
    public String getSignup(Model model, Locale locale,
        @ModelAttribute SignupForm form) {
      …(Omitted)
    }

    /** User signup process */
    @PostMapping("/signup")
    public String postSignup(Model model, Locale locale,
        @ModelAttribute @Validated(GroupOrder.class) SignupForm form,
        BindingResult bindingResult) {
      …(Omitted)
    }

    /** Database-related exception handling */
    @ExceptionHandler(DataAccessException.class)
    public String dataAccessExceptionHandler(DataAccessException e, Model model) {
      // Set an empty string
      model.addAttribute("error", "");

      // Register message in Model
      model.addAttribute("message", "An exception occurred in SignupController");

      // Register HTTP error code(500) in Model
```

```
        model.addAttribute("status", HttpStatus.INTERNAL_SERVER_ERROR);

        return "error";
    }

    /** Other exception handling */
    @ExceptionHandler(Exception.class)
    public String exceptionHandler(Exception e, Model model) {
        // Set an empty string
        model.addAttribute("error", "");

        // Register message in Model
        model.addAttribute("message", "An exception occurred in SignupController");

        // Register HTTP error code(500) in Model
        model.addAttribute("status", HttpStatus.INTERNAL_SERVER_ERROR);

        return "error";
    }
}
```

Point: @ExceptionHandler

Exception handling can be implemented by providing a method with the @ExceptionHandler annotation. Specify the exception class in the argument of the annotation. This allows you to handle each exception. Also, you can prepare multiple methods with @ExceptionHandler.

In the sample code above, the common error screen is displayed when an exception occurs. At that time, error messages and other information are registered in the Model class.

Execution

Run SpringBoot to access the user signup screen.

Enter "system@co.jp" in the User ID field to register the user. A unique constraint violation occurs.

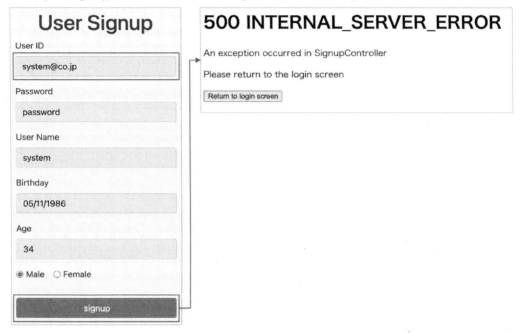

The Common Errors page is displayed. The exception handling message you just created is displayed.

10.2.3 Exception handling for the entire web application

Overview

If you prepare exception handling for each controller class, you can handle exceptions appropriately for each screen. However, it is possible for someone to forget to implement exception handling. Therefore, prepare exception handling for the entire Web application. This allows you to implement exception handling in bulk.

When exception handling is executed for the entire web application, the following message is displayed on the common error page.

[Common error page]

500 INTERNAL_SERVER_ERROR

Exception has occurred

Please return to the login screen

Return to login screen

Directory

The directory structure is as follows. The part where the background color is changed is the new part to be added.

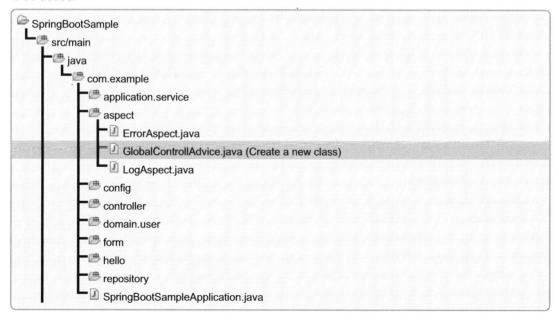

```
┣▣ resources
  ┗▣ pom.xml
```

Source Code

Create exception handling for the entire web application.
[GlobalControllAdvice.java]

```java
package com.example.aspect;

import org.springframework.dao.DataAccessException;
import org.springframework.http.HttpStatus;
import org.springframework.stereotype.Component;
import org.springframework.ui.Model;
import org.springframework.web.bind.annotation.ControllerAdvice;
import org.springframework.web.bind.annotation.ExceptionHandler;


@ControllerAdvice
public class GlobalControllAdvice {

    /** Database-related exception handling */
    @ExceptionHandler(DataAccessException.class)
    public String dataAccessExceptionHandler(DataAccessException e, Model model) {
        // Set an empty string
        model.addAttribute("error", "");

        // Register message in Model
        model.addAttribute("message", "DataAccessException has occurred");

        // Register HTTP error code(500) in Model
        model.addAttribute("status", HttpStatus.INTERNAL_SERVER_ERROR);

        return "error";
    }

    /** Other exception handling */
    @ExceptionHandler(Exception.class)
    public String exceptionHandler(Exception e, Model model) {
        // Set an empty string
        model.addAttribute("error", "");

        // Register message in Model
        model.addAttribute("message", "Exception has occurred");

        // Register HTTP error code(500) in Model
        model.addAttribute("status", HttpStatus.INTERNAL_SERVER_ERROR);

        return "error";
```

```
    }
}
```

Point: @ControllerAdvice

By attaching this annotation to the class, you can prepare a method that is shared by all controllers. However, only methods with one of the following annotations can be shared between controllers.

- @ExceptionHandler
- @InitBinder
- @ModelAttribute

Execution

Run Spring Boot and access the following URL.

[URL]

http://localhost:8080/user/detail

When accessing the user details screen, an error will occur if the user ID is not included in the URL. Therefore, the screen will change to the common error screen.

[Common error screen

500 INTERNAL_SERVER_ERROR

Exception has occurred

Please return to the login screen

Return to login screen

Summary

Here's what you've learned in this chapter:

[Error screen]

- To create a common error screen, prepare "error.html".
- Prepare an error screen file under "src/main/resources/templates/error". If you have a file called "404.html", you can create a page for 404 errors.

[Exception Handling]

There are three ways to handle exceptions:

- Use the @AfterThrowing annotation.
- The @ExceptionHandler annotation is used for exception handling per controller class.
- The @ControllerAdvice and @ExceptionHandler annotations are used to handle exceptions throughout the web application.

11. Spring Security

In this chapter, you'll learn about Spring security. Security is an essential feature of web applications. You will learn about the following contents.

- Overview
- Authentication
- Authorization

11.1 Overview

Spring security has authentication and authorization features.

Authentication is simply a login feature. Only users who have successfully logged in can use the various functions. Spring makes it very easy to create login features.

Authorization is a function restriction by authority. In Spring, various functions can be restricted by the authority that the user has. For example, you can block access to specific URLs. You can also change the screen display items depending on the authority.

You will learn about these functions while actually making them.

11.2 Authentication

First, create the login function. You will create it in the following order.

- Prohibition of direct link
- Login process
- In-Memory authentication
- Password encryption
- User data authentication
- Logout processing
- CSRF measures

11.2.1 Prohibition of direct link

Overview

If you can access the screen by directly entering the URL, there is no point in creating a login function. It's like building a gate without a wall around the house.

Therefore, except for some screens, users cannot access the screen without logging in. In other words, direct links are prohibited. If the user is not logged in and tries to access the screen, the screen will change to the common error screen.

[Common error screen]

403 Forbidden

Access Denied

Please return to the login screen

Return to login screen

Directory

The directory structure is as follows. The part where the background color is changed is the new part to be added.

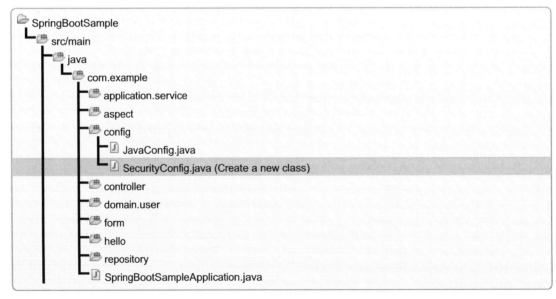

```
    resources
    pom.xml
```

Source Code

First, add a library of Spring security. Add the following code in the dependencies tag of pom.xml. The part where the background color is changed is the added part.

[pom.xml]

```xml
<dependencies>
  …
  <!-- SpringSecurity -->
  <dependency>
    <groupId>org.springframework.boot</groupId>
    <artifactId>spring-boot-starter-security</artifactId>
  </dependency>
  <!-- Thyemeleaf Extension Library (Security) -->
  <dependency>
    <groupId>org.thymeleaf.extras</groupId>
    <artifactId>thymeleaf-extras-springsecurity5</artifactId>
  </dependency>
  …
</dependencies>
```

Next, prepare a security configuration class.

[SecurityConfig.java]

```java
package com.example.config;

import org.springframework.context.annotation.Configuration;
import org.springframework.security.config.annotation.web.builders.HttpSecurity;
import org.springframework.security.config.annotation.web.builders.WebSecurity;
import org.springframework.security.config.annotation.web.configuration.EnableWebSecurity;
import org.springframework.security.config.annotation.web.configuration.WebSecurityConfigurerAdapter;

@EnableWebSecurity
@Configuration
public class SecurityConfig extends WebSecurityConfigurerAdapter {

    /** Set a target out-of-security */
    @Override
    public void configure(WebSecurity web) throws Exception {
        // Do not apply security
        web
            .ignoring()
                .antMatchers("/webjars/**")
                .antMatchers("/css/**")
```

```
            .antMatchers("/js/**")
            .antMatchers("/h2-console/**");
    }

    /** Various security settings */
    @Override
    protected void configure(HttpSecurity http) throws Exception {
        // Set of login unnecessary page
        http
            .authorizeRequests()
                .antMatchers("/login").permitAll() //Direct link OK
                .antMatchers("/user/signup").permitAll() //Direct link OK
                .anyRequest().authenticated(); // Otherwise direct link NG

        // Disable CSRF measures (temporary)
        http.csrf().disable();
    }
}
```

Point 1: Security Configuration Class

To prepare the security setting class, make the following settings.

- Annotate the class with @Configuration and @EnableWebSecurity.
- Inherit the WebSecurityConfigurerAdapter class.

You can change the security settings by overriding the methods of the WebSecurityConfigureAdapter.

Point2: Excluded from the security target

Make static resources such as webjars and css accessible to everyone. It also allows you to use the H2 database console without logging in. Therefore, these resources are excluded from security. The setting method is as follows.

[How to Configure Security Exclusions]

```
web.ignoring().antMatchers("Excluded path")
```

The antMatchers method can use the method chain as in the sample code.

Point3: Prohibition of direct link

To prohibit direct links, use the http.authorizeRequests method. After this method, you will add settings for each path.

[Direct link: OK]

```
antMatchers("path").permitAll()
```

Specify the path in the argument of the antMatchers method. Use the permitAll method to allow access to that path without authenticating.

[Direct link: NG]

```
anyRequest().authenticated()
```

All paths are targeted by the anyRequest method. The authenticated method requires authentication. This means that "anyRequest().authenticated()" requires authentication on all paths.

These settings are applied in the order in which they are called in the method chain. Therefore, if "anyRequest().authenticated()" is set first, authentication is required for all screens.

In addition to prohibiting direct links, CSRF measures are disabled. This will be explained in [11.2.7 CSRF Countermeasures].

Execution

Run Spring Boot and access the following URL.

[URL]

http://localhost:8080/user/list

Attempt to display the user list screen. However, because you are not logged in, you will see a common error screen.

[Common error screen]

403 Forbidden

Access Denied

Please return to the login screen

Return to login screen

HTTP403 is an error code that prohibits access.

Note: When the screen is displayed

If the screen such as the user list is displayed without the 403 error, clear the cache or clean the project.

The execution result is omitted, but the login screen and user signup screen are displayed even if you do not log in.

11.2.2 Login process

Overview

Click the "Login" button without entering user ID and password on the login screen. Since you are trying to transition to the user list screen without authenticating, the screen will transition to the common error screen.

Due to the prohibition of direct links, various screens cannot be displayed without logging in. So, first we will create the basis for the login function. After pressing the "login" button, set to use the login function.

[Login Screen] (Login Failed)

※You cannot log in yet.

Directory

There is no change in the directory structure.

Source Code

First, modify the security configuration class. The part where the background color is changed is the modified part.

[SecurityConfig.java]

```java
@EnableWebSecurity
@Configuration
public class SecurityConfig extends WebSecurityConfigurerAdapter {

    /** Set a target out-of-security */
    @Override
    public void configure(WebSecurity web) throws Exception {
        ...(Omitted)
    }

    /** Various security settings */
    @Override
    protected void configure(HttpSecurity http) throws Exception {
        // Set of login unnecessary page
        http
            .authorizeRequests()
                .antMatchers("/login").permitAll() //Direct link OK
                .antMatchers("/user/signup").permitAll() //Direct link OK
                .anyRequest().authenticated(); // Otherwise direct link NG

        // Login process
        http
            .formLogin()
                .loginProcessingUrl("/login") // Login process path
                .loginPage("/login") // Specify login page
                .failureUrl("/login?error") // Transition destination when login fails
                .usernameParameter("userId") // Login page user ID
                .passwordParameter("password") // Login page password
                .defaultSuccessUrl("/user/list", true); // Transition destination after success

        // Disable CSRF measures (temporary)
        http.csrf().disable();
    }
}
```

Point: Login Processing

To add a login process, call the http.formLogin method. From that method, add a condition in the method chain.

- **loginProcessingUrl("path")**

    Specify the path for login processing. Match the path with the [th:action="@{/login}"] part of the form tag in the html of the login screen.

- **loginPage("path")**
  Set the link destination of the login page. If you don't set this, you'll see the default login page provided by Spring Security. Match the path with the @GetMapping ("/login") part of the controller on the login screen.

- **failureUrl("path")**
  Transition destination when login fails.

- **userNameParameter("the name attribute of User ID")**
  Set the value of the name attribute in the user ID input field on the login screen.

- **passwordParameter("the name attribute of password")**
  Set the value of the name attribute in the password input field on the login screen.

- **defaultSuccessUrl("Transition destination path after successful login", Whether to transition to the transition destination of the first argument)**
  Specify the transition destination after successful login. If you specify true for the second argument, you will be forced to transition to the path of the first argument.

Then modify the login screen. The part where the background color is changed is the modified part.
[login.html]

```html
<!DOCTYPE html>
<html xmlns:th="http://www.thymeleaf.org">
<head>
 …(Omitted)
</head>
<body class="bg-light">
 <div class="text-center">
  <form method="post" th:action="@{/login}" class="form-login">
   <h2>Login</h2>
   <p th:if="${session['SPRING_SECURITY_LAST_EXCEPTION']} != null"
    th:text="${session['SPRING_SECURITY_LAST_EXCEPTION'].message}"
    class="text-danger">
   Login error message
   </p>
   <!-- User ID -->
   <div class="form-group">
    <label for="userId" class="sr-only">userId</label>
    <input type="text" class="form-control" placeholder="User ID"
      name="userId"/>
   </div>
   <!-- Password -->
   <div class="form-group">
    <label for="password" class="sr-only">password</label>
    <input type="text" class="form-control" placeholder="Password"
```

```
        name="password"/>
    </div>
    <input type="submit" value="Login" class="btn btn-primary" />
    </form>
    <a th:href="@{/user/signup}">Signup</a>
  </div>
</body>
</html>
```

Point: Login Error Message

To display the login error message, write the same code as the sample code. If there is a security error in the session, an error message will be displayed.

Execution

Run SpringBoot to access the login screen. On the login screen, click the Login button.

[Login Screen]

The transition to the common error screen will not occur. Then, an error message will be displayed on the login screen.

11.2.3 In-Memory authentication

Overview

Next, create an in-memory authentication. In-memory authentication is a function that allows you to log in by preparing a temporary user ID and password. This feature allows you to log in without a user table or data. As a result, security will not stop development.

Directory

There is no change in the directory structure.

Source Code

Modify the security configuration class. The part where the background color is changed is the modified part.

[SecurityConfig.java]

```java
package com.example.config;

import org.springframework.context.annotation.Configuration;
import org.springframework.security.config.annotation.authentication.builders.AuthenticationManagerBuilder;
import org.springframework.security.config.annotation.web.builders.HttpSecurity;
import org.springframework.security.config.annotation.web.builders.WebSecurity;
import org.springframework.security.config.annotation.web.configuration.EnableWebSecurity;
import org.springframework.security.config.annotation.web.configuration.WebSecurityConfigurerAdapter;

@EnableWebSecurity
@Configuration
public class SecurityConfig extends WebSecurityConfigurerAdapter {

    /** Set a target out-of-security */
    @Override
    public void configure(WebSecurity web) throws Exception {
        ...(Omitted)
    }

    /** Various security settings */
    @Override
    protected void configure(HttpSecurity http) throws Exception {
        ...(Omitted)
    }

    /** Authentication settings */
    @Override
```

```
protected void configure(AuthenticationManagerBuilder auth) throws Exception {
    // In-memory authentication
    auth
      .inMemoryAuthentication()
        .withUser("user") // add user
          .password("user")
          .roles("GENERAL")
        .and()
        .withUser("admin") // add admin
          .password("admin")
          .roles("ADMIN");
  }
}
```

Point: In-Memory authentication

You can create in-memory authentication using the auth.inMemoryAuthentication() method. After the inMemoryAuthentication() method, call the following method to add the user.

- withUser("User ID")
- password("Password")
- roles("Role name")

You can add multiple users by connecting these methods with the "and" method.

Then modify the message properties to change the message when login fails. The part where the background color is changed is the modified part.

[messages.properties]

```
user.signup.title=User Signup
user.signup.btn=signup
userId=User ID
password=Password
userName=User Name
birthday=Birthday
age=Age
male=Male
female=Female
gender=Gondor

# =================
# Login failure message
# =================
AbstractUserDetailsAuthenticationProvider.locked=Account is locked
AbstractUserDetailsAuthenticationProvider.disabled=Account is not available
AbstractUserDetailsAuthenticationProvider.expired=Account has expired
AbstractUserDetailsAuthenticationProvider.credentialsExpired=Password has expired
AbstractUserDetailsAuthenticationProvider.badCredentials=ID or password is incorrect
```

With Spring Security, you can do various checks when you log in. In the sample code, the message corresponding to those checks is changed. However, the samples in this book only display the message "ID or password is incorrect".

Execution

Run SpringBoot to access the login screen. Try logging in with the user ID and password that you set for in-memory authentication.

[Login screen]

The error message has changed, but the login still fails. This is because Spring security requires password encryption.

11.2.4 Password encryption

Overview

In this section, you will learn how to create password encryption.

Create the following process.

- Encrypt passwords for in-memory authenticated users.
- Encrypt the password for user registration / update.

This will allow you to log in with in-memory authentication.

Directory

There is no change in the directory structure.

Source Code

Modify the security configuration class. The part where the background color is changed is the modified part.

[SecurityConfig.java]

```java
package com.example.config;

import org.springframework.context.annotation.Bean;
import org.springframework.context.annotation.Configuration;
import org.springframework.security.config.annotation.authentication.builders.AuthenticationManagerBuilder;
import org.springframework.security.config.annotation.web.builders.HttpSecurity;
import org.springframework.security.config.annotation.web.builders.WebSecurity;
import org.springframework.security.config.annotation.web.configuration.EnableWebSecurity;
import org.springframework.security.config.annotation.web.configuration.WebSecurityConfigurerAdapter;
import org.springframework.security.crypto.bcrypt.BCryptPasswordEncoder;
import org.springframework.security.crypto.password.PasswordEncoder;

@EnableWebSecurity
@Configuration
public class SecurityConfig extends WebSecurityConfigurerAdapter {

    @Bean
    public PasswordEncoder passwordEncoder() {
        return new BCryptPasswordEncoder();
    }

    /** Set a target out-of-security */
    @Override
```

```
public void configure(WebSecurity web) throws Exception {
    ...(Omitted)
}

/** Various security settings */
@Override
protected void configure(HttpSecurity http) throws Exception {
    ...(Omitted)
}

/** Authentication settings */
@Override
protected void configure(AuthenticationManagerBuilder auth) throws Exception {

    PasswordEncoder encoder = passwordEncoder();
    // In-memory authentication
    auth
        .inMemoryAuthentication()
            .withUser("user") // add user
                .password(encoder.encode("user"))
                .roles("GENERAL")
            .and()
            .withUser("admin") // add admin
                .password(encoder.encode("admin"))
                .roles("ADMIN");
    }
}
```

Point: Password Encryption

The PasswordEncoder interface is provided by Spring. This is the interface for encrypting passwords. Various implementation classes are provided depending on the encryption algorithm. Among them, the use of BCryptPasswordEncoder, which hashes passwords, is recommended. This is because even if the password is stolen, it is difficult to decrypt it.

In the sample code, the user password prepared by in-memory authentication is encrypted.

Next, the password is encrypted when the user is registered / updated. Modify the user service implementation class. The part where the background color is changed is the modified part.

[UserServiceImpl.java]

```
package com.example.domain.user.service.impl;

import java.util.List;

import org.springframework.beans.factory.annotation.Autowired;
import org.springframework.security.crypto.password.PasswordEncoder;
import org.springframework.stereotype.Service;
import org.springframework.transaction.annotation.Transactional;
```

```
import com.example.domain.user.model.MUser;
import com.example.domain.user.service.UserService;
import com.example.repository.UserMapper;

@Service
public class UserServiceImpl implements UserService {

    @Autowired
    private UserMapper mapper;

    @Autowired
    private PasswordEncoder encoder;

    /** User signup */
    @Override
    public void signup(MUser user) {
        user.setDepartmentId(1);
        user.setRole("ROLE_GENERAL");

        // Password encryption
        String rawPassword = user.getPassword();
        user.setPassword(encoder.encode(rawPassword));

        mapper.insertOne(user);
    }

    /** Get user */
    @Override
    public List<MUser> getUsers(MUser user) {
        return mapper.findMany(user);
    }

    /** Get user(1record) */
    @Override
    public MUser getUserOne(String userId) {
        return mapper.findOne(userId);
    }

    /** Update user */
    @Transactional
    @Override
    public void updateUserOne(String userId,
        String password,
        String userName) {

        // Password encryption
        String encryptPassword = encoder.encode(password);

        mapper.updateOne(userId, encryptPassword, userName);

        // Raise an exception
```

```
    // int i = 1 / 0;
  }

  /** Delete user */
  @Override
  public void deleteUserOne(String userId) {
    int count = mapper.deleteOne(userId);
  }
}
```

Execution

Run SpringBoot and access the login screen. Log in with the user ID and password prepared for in-memory authentication.

[Login screen]

The login is successful and the user list screen is displayed. (The execution result is omitted).

11.2.5 User data authentication

Overview

Modify the application so that it can be authenticated using the data in the user master.

Directory

The directory structure is as follows. The part where the background color is changed is the new part to be added.

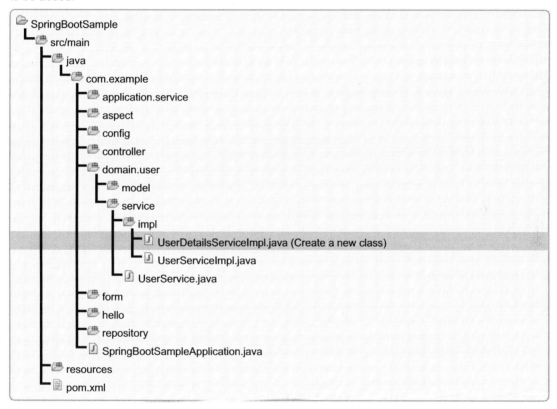

Source Code

Prepare the SQL to get the login user information. First, modify the mapper.The part where the background color is changed is the modified part.

[UserMapper.java]

```java
package com.example.repository;

import java.util.List;

import org.apache.ibatis.annotations.Mapper;
import org.apache.ibatis.annotations.Param;

import com.example.domain.user.model.MUser;

@Mapper
public interface UserMapper {

    /** User signup */
    public int insertOne(MUser user);

    /** Get user */
    public List<MUser> findMany(MUser user);

    /** Get user(1record) */
    public MUser findOne(String userId);

    /** Update user */
    public void updateOne(@Param("userId") String userId,
        @Param("password") String password,
        @Param("userName") String userName);

    /** Delete user */
    public int deleteOne(@Param("userId") String userId);

    /** Get login user */
    public MUser findLoginUser(String userId);
}
```

Then modify xml. The part where the background color is changed is the modified part.

[UserMapper.xml]

```xml
<?xml version="1.0" encoding="UTF-8"?>
<!DOCTYPE mapper PUBLIC "-//mybatis.org//DTD Mapper 3.0//EN"
 "http://mybatis.org/dtd/mybatis-3-mapper.dtd">

<!-- Mapper and xml mapping -->
<mapper namespace="com.example.repository.UserMapper">
```

```xml
<!-- Mapping definition (user) -->
<resultMap type="com.example.domain.user.model.MUser" id="user">
    …(Omitted)
</resultMap>

<!-- Mapping definition (department) -->
<resultMap type="com.example.domain.user.model.Department" id="department">
    …(Omitted)
</resultMap>

<!-- Mapping definition (salary) -->
<resultMap type="com.example.domain.user.model.Salary" id="salary">
    …(Omitted)
</resultMap>

<!-- user registration -->
<insert id="insertOne">
    …(Omitted)
</insert>

<!-- Get user(multiple) -->
<select id="findMany" resultType="MUser">
    …(Omitted)
</select>

<!-- Get user(1record) -->
<select id="findOne" resultMap="user">
    …(Omitted)
</select>

<!-- Update user -->
<update id="updateOne">
    …(Omitted)
</update>

<!-- Delete user -->
<delete id="deleteOne">
    …(Omitted)
</delete>

<!-- Get login user information -->
<select id="findLoginUser" resultType="MUser">
    select
      *
    from
      m_user
    where
      user_id = #{userId}
</select>
</mapper>
```

Then modify the user service. The part where the background color is changed is the modified part.

[UserService.java]

```
public interface UserService {

  /** User signup */
  public void signup(MUser user);

  /** Get user */
  public List<MUser> getUsers(MUser user);

  /** Get user(1record) */
  public MUser getUserOne(String userId);

  /** Update user */
  public void updateUserOne(String userId,
      String password,
      String userName);

  /** Delete user */
  public void deleteUserOne(String userId);

  /** Get login user information */
  public MUser getLoginUser(String userId);
}
```

Also modify the user service implementation class. The part where the background color is changed is the modified part.

[UserServiceImpl.java]

```
@Service
public class UserServiceImpl implements UserService {

  @Autowired
  private UserMapper mapper;

  /** User signup */
  @Override
  public void signup(MUser user) {
    ...(Omitted)
  }

  /** Get user */
  @Override
  public List<MUser> getUsers(MUser user) {
    return mapper.findMany(user);
  }

  /** Get user(1record) */
  @Override
```

```
    public MUser getUserOne(String userId) {
        return mapper.findOne(userId);
    }

    /** Update user */
    @Transactional
    @Override
    public void updateUserOne(String userId,
        String password,
        String userName) {
        …(Omitted)
    }

    /** Delete user */
    @Override
    public void deleteUserOne(String userId) {
        int count = mapper.deleteOne(userId);
    }

    /** Get login user information */
    @Override
    public MUser getLoginUser(String userId) {
        return mapper.findLoginUser(userId);
    }
}
```

Next, create a service to use for login authentication.
[UserDetailsServiceImpl.java]

```
package com.example.domain.user.service.impl;

import java.util.ArrayList;
import java.util.List;

import org.springframework.beans.factory.annotation.Autowired;
import org.springframework.security.core.GrantedAuthority;
import org.springframework.security.core.authority.SimpleGrantedAuthority;
import org.springframework.security.core.userdetails.User;
import org.springframework.security.core.userdetails.UserDetails;
import org.springframework.security.core.userdetails.UserDetailsService;
import org.springframework.security.core.userdetails.UsernameNotFoundException;
import org.springframework.stereotype.Service;

import com.example.domain.login.model.MUser;
import com.example.domain.user.service.UserService;

@Service
public class UserDetailsServiceImpl implements UserDetailsService {

    @Autowired
```

```java
    private UserService service;

    @Override
    public UserDetails loadUserByUsername(String username)
        throws UsernameNotFoundException {

        // Get user information
        MUser loginUser = service.getLoginUser(username);

        // If the user does not exist
        if (loginUser == null) {
            throw new UsernameNotFoundException("user not found");
        }

        // Create authority list
        GrantedAuthority authority = new SimpleGrantedAuthority(loginUser.getRole());
        List<GrantedAuthority> authorities = new ArrayList<>();
        authorities.add(authority);

        // Generate UserDetails
        UserDetails userDetails = (UserDetails) new User(loginUser.getUserId(),
            loginUser.getPassword(),
            authorities);

        return userDetails;
    }
}
```

Point: UserDetailsService

To create a user authentication service, prepare a class that implements UserDetailsService.

Then override the loadUserByUsername method. The return value of this method is the UserDetails interface. This interface represents the user. The sample code generates "org.springframework.security.core.userdetails.User", which is an implementation class of UserDetails.

To generate UserDetails, the user ID, password, and authorization list are required.

Finally, modify the security configuration class. The part where the background color is changed is the modified part.

[SecurityConfig.java]

```java
package com.example.config;

import org.springframework.beans.factory.annotation.Autowired;
import org.springframework.context.annotation.Bean;
import org.springframework.context.annotation.Configuration;
```

```java
import org.springframework.security.config.annotation.authentication.builders.AuthenticationManagerBuilder;
import org.springframework.security.config.annotation.web.builders.HttpSecurity;
import org.springframework.security.config.annotation.web.builders.WebSecurity;
import org.springframework.security.config.annotation.web.configuration.EnableWebSecurity;
import org.springframework.security.config.annotation.web.configuration.WebSecurityConfigurerAdapter;
import org.springframework.security.core.userdetails.UserDetailsService;
import org.springframework.security.crypto.bcrypt.BCryptPasswordEncoder;
import org.springframework.security.crypto.password.PasswordEncoder;


@EnableWebSecurity
@Configuration
public class SecurityConfig extends WebSecurityConfigurerAdapter {

    @Autowired
    private UserDetailsService userDetailsService;

    @Bean
    public PasswordEncoder passwordEncoder() {
        return new BCryptPasswordEncoder();
    }

    /** Set a target out-of-security */
    @Override
    public void configure(WebSecurity web) throws Exception {
        …(Omitted)
    }

    /** Various security settings */
    @Override
    protected void configure(HttpSecurity http) throws Exception {
        …(Omitted)
    }

    /** Authentication settings */
    @Override
    protected void configure(AuthenticationManagerBuilder auth) throws Exception {

        PasswordEncoder encoder = passwordEncoder();
        // In-memory authentication
        /*
        auth
            .inMemoryAuthentication()
                .withUser("user") // add user
                    .password(encoder.encode("user"))
                    .roles("GENERAL")
                .and()
                .withUser("admin") // add admin
                    .password(encoder.encode("admin"))
                    .roles("ADMIN");
        */
```

```
    // User data authentication
    auth
        .userDetailsService(userDetailsService)
        .passwordEncoder(encoder);
    }
}
```

Point: User data authentication

To authenticate user data, use the "auth.userDetailsService" method. Set your own UserDetailsService in the argument of this method. Also, password encryption is required, so use the passwordEncoder method.

Since the in-memory authentication is no longer used, it has been commented out.

Execution

Run SpringBoot and access the user signup screen. First, register the user. At that time, please set "password" in the password input field. After registering the user, check the console screen of the H2 database.

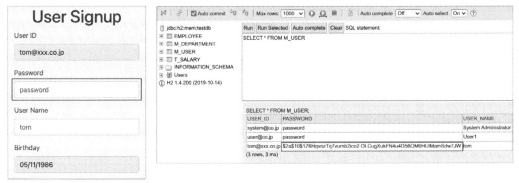

The registered user's password is encrypted. Set that password to the password of the initial input user. The values generated are different each time, but that's okay.

[data.sql]

```
/* User master */
INSERT INTO m_user (
    user_id
    , password
    , user_name
    , birthday
    , age
    , gender
) VALUES
('system@co.jp', '$2a$10$1Z6HqvozTq7vurnb2ico2.OLCugXukFN4u4D56OM6HUlMamSdw7JW', 'System Adminis
trator', '2000-01-01', 21, 1, 1, 'ROLE_ADMIN')
```

, ('user@co.jp', '$2a$10$1Z6HqvozTq7vurnb2ico2.OLCugXukFN4u4D56OM6HUlMamSdw7JW', 'User1', '2000-0
1-01', 21, 2, 2, 'ROLE_GENERAL')
;

You are now ready to log in with user data. Restart SpringBoot and log in as the initial data user.

[User data]

User ID	Password
system@co.jp	password
user@co.jp	password

[Login screen]

If the login is successful, the user list screen will be displayed. (The execution result is omitted).

11.2.6 Logout processing

Overview

After creating the login process, let's also create the logout process.

Directory

There is no change in the directory structure.

Source Code

Modify the security configuration class. The part where the background color is changed is the modified part.

[SecurityConfig.java]

```java
package com.example.config;

import org.springframework.beans.factory.annotation.Autowired;
import org.springframework.context.annotation.Bean;
import org.springframework.context.annotation.Configuration;
import org.springframework.security.config.annotation.authentication.builders.AuthenticationManagerBuilder;
import org.springframework.security.config.annotation.web.builders.HttpSecurity;
import org.springframework.security.config.annotation.web.builders.WebSecurity;
import org.springframework.security.config.annotation.web.configuration.EnableWebSecurity;
import org.springframework.security.config.annotation.web.configuration.WebSecurityConfigurerAdapter;
import org.springframework.security.core.userdetails.UserDetailsService;
import org.springframework.security.crypto.bcrypt.BCryptPasswordEncoder;
import org.springframework.security.crypto.password.PasswordEncoder;
import org.springframework.security.web.util.matcher.AntPathRequestMatcher;

@EnableWebSecurity
@Configuration
public class SecurityConfig extends WebSecurityConfigurerAdapter {

    @Autowired
    private UserDetailsService userDetailsService;

    @Bean
    public PasswordEncoder passwordEncoder() {
        return new BCryptPasswordEncoder();
    }

    /** Set a target out-of-security */
    @Override
    public void configure(WebSecurity web) throws Exception {
```

```
    …(Omitted)
}

/** Various security settings */
@Override
protected void configure(HttpSecurity http) throws Exception {
    // Set of login unnecessary page
    http
        .authorizeRequests()
            .antMatchers("/login").permitAll() //Direct link OK
            .antMatchers("/user/signup").permitAll() //Direct link OK
            .anyRequest().authenticated(); // Otherwise direct link NG

    // Login process
    http
        .formLogin()
            .loginProcessingUrl("/login") // Login process path
            .loginPage("/login") // Specify login page
            .failureUrl("/login?error") // Transition destination when login fails
            .usernameParameter("userId") // Login page user ID
            .passwordParameter("password") // Login page password
            .defaultSuccessUrl("/user/list", true); // Transition destination after success

    // Logout process
    http
        .logout()
            .logoutRequestMatcher(new AntPathRequestMatcher("/logout"))
            .logoutUrl("/logout")
            .logoutSuccessUrl("/login?logout");

    // Disable CSRF measures (temporary)
    http.csrf().disable();
}

/** Authentication settings */
@Override
protected void configure(AuthenticationManagerBuilder auth) throws Exception {
    …(Omitted)
}
}
```

Point: Logout Processing

Use the following method to set the logout process.

- **logoutRequestMatcher()**

  By default in Spring, the logout process is sent by the POST method. If you want to send a logout request with the GET method, add this method. In this book, I put in for reference.

- **logoutUrl("path")**

  Set the logout request path. That is, match the path of [th:action="@{/logout}"] in the HTML file with the setting value of this method. This method is the setting when logging out with the POST method.

- **logoutSuccessUrl("path")**

  Specify the transition destination when logout is successful.

Execution

Run SpringBoot and log in. Click the "Logout" button from the user list screen.

[User list screen]

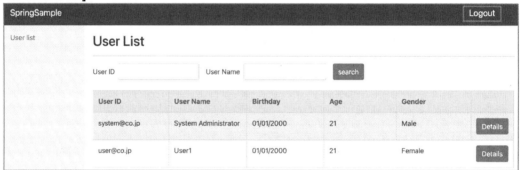

If you move to the login screen and the following URL is displayed, you have successfully logged out.

[URL after logout]

http://localhost:8080/login?logout

Note: No logout controller required

Since the Spring Security will do a logout process, log out of the controller is no longer required. Even if the comment out the code of the log out controller, logout processing is done. Until now, the logout controller was used only for screen transitions.

11.2.7 CSRF measures

Overview

First, I will explain what CSRF measures are.

[What is CSRF?]

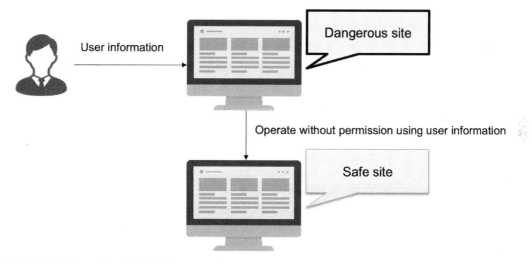

What kind of attack is CSRF? It is to send a request that the user does not intend to the website. For example, create a site where bad people win a lot of money by lottery. The site will prompt you for your personal information. The personal information will allow you to access another website. And you will be forced to buy expensive items without permission.

Is an acronym for cross-site request forgery (Cross Site Request Forgeries), it referred to as CSRF.

[What is CSRF measures?]

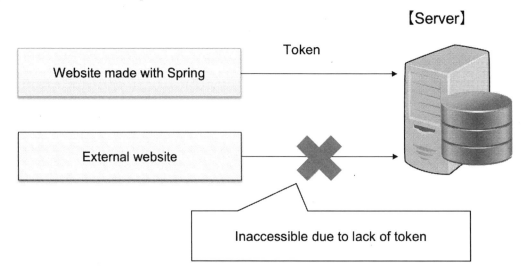

To prevent CSRF, websites created with Spring will now include tokens. A token is a random string.

If you send a request without a token, it will be considered as an external request. As a result, the request is rejected. This token is required when making a request using a method other than GET. It is not necessary to include the token in the parameter, such as when displaying the screen with the GET method.

With Spring security included, CSRF measures is enabled by default. Until now, CSRF measures have been disabled for learning purposes. In this section, you will enable CSRF measures.

Directory

There is no change in the directory structure.

Source Code

Modify the security configuration class to enable CSRF measures. The part where the background color is changed is the modified part.
[SecurityConfig.java]

```
@EnableWebSecurity
@Configuration
public class SecurityConfig extends WebSecurityConfigurerAdapter {

    @Autowired
    private UserDetailsService userDetailsService;

    @Bean
```

```java
public PasswordEncoder passwordEncoder() {
    return new BCryptPasswordEncoder();
}


/** Set a target out-of-security */
@Override
public void configure(WebSecurity web) throws Exception {
    …(Omitted)
}


/** Various security settings */
@Override
protected void configure(HttpSecurity http) throws Exception {
    // Set of login unnecessary page
    http
        .authorizeRequests()
            .antMatchers("/login").permitAll() //Direct link OK
            .antMatchers("/user/signup").permitAll() //Direct link OK
            .anyRequest().authenticated(); // Otherwise direct link NG


    // Login process
    http
        .formLogin()
            .loginProcessingUrl("/login") // Login process path
            .loginPage("/login") // Specify login page
            .failureUrl("/login?error") // Transition destination when login fails
            .usernameParameter("userId") // Login page user ID
            .passwordParameter("password") // Login page password
            .defaultSuccessUrl("/user/list", true); // Transition destination after success


    // Logout process
    http
        .logout()
            .logoutRequestMatcher(new AntPathRequestMatcher("/logout"))
            .logoutUrl("/logout")
            .logoutSuccessUrl("/login?logout");


    // Disable CSRF measures (temporary)
    // http.csrf().disable();
}


/** Authentication settings */
@Override
protected void configure(AuthenticationManagerBuilder auth) throws Exception {
    …(Omitted)
}
}
```

Next, modify the user signup screen to send the CSRF token. The part where the background color is changed is the modified part.

[signup.html]

```html
<!DOCTYPE html>
<html xmlns:th="http://www.thymeleaf.org">
<head>
 ...(Omitted)
</head>
<body class="bg-light">
 <form id="signup-form" method="post" action="/user/signup"
   class="form-signup" th:object="${signupForm}">
  <h1 class="text-center" th:text="#{user.signup.title}"></h1>
  <!-- User ID -->
  <div class="form-group">
   ...(Omitted)
  </div>
  <!-- Password -->
  <div class="form-group" >
   ...(Omitted)
  </div>
  <!-- User Name -->
  <div class="form-group">
   ...(Omitted)
  </div>
  <!-- Birthday -->
  <div class="form-group">
   ...(Omitted)
  </div>
  <!-- Age -->
  <div class="form-group">
   ...(Omitted)
  </div>
  <!-- Gender -->
  <div class="form-group">
   ...(Omitted)
  <div>
  <!-- Signup button -->
  <input type="submit" th:value="#{user.signup.btn}"
    class="btn btn-primary w-100 mt-3" />
  <input type="hidden" th:name="${_csrf.parameterName}"
    th:value="${_csrf.token}" />
 </form>
</body>
</html>
```

Point: CSRF token

To send a CSRF token, add the above code inside the form tag.

Execution

Run SpringBoot and access the user signup screen. Please register the user.

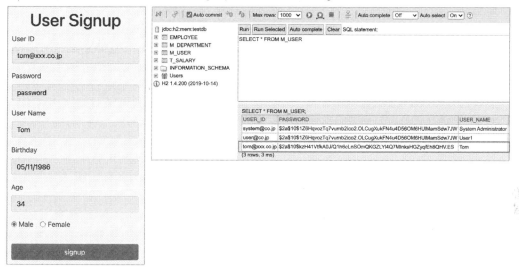

After registering as a user, check the console screen of the H2 database. If the user is registered, the request has been authenticated. If you comment out the CSRF token, the user will not be registered.

Note: "th:action"

Don't you need CSRF tokens on other screens? You might have thought. The POST method is also used to update / delete users.

However, you do not need to add the CSRF token to the parameter on other screens. This is because other screens use the "th:action" attribute in the form tag. If you use this attribute, the CSRF token parameters will be added automatically. Only the user registration screen was intentionally set to the "action" attribute instead of the "th:action" attribute.

Be sure to use the "th:action" tag when creating a screen with Spring.

11.3 Authorization

After learned about authentication, we will learn about the authorization.

- URL authorization
- Screen display authorization

11.3.1 URL authorization

Overview

Set the specified URL so that unauthorized users cannot access it. First, prepare a link to the admin permission screen in the menu.

[Menu after login]

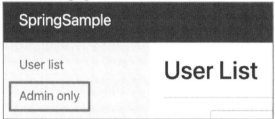

The admin authority only screen is a screen that only confirms access control by authority.

[Admin authority only screen]

If you try to access this screen as an unauthorized user, you will be taken to the common error screen.

[Common error screen]

Directory

The directory structure is as follows. The part where the background color is changed is the new part to be added.

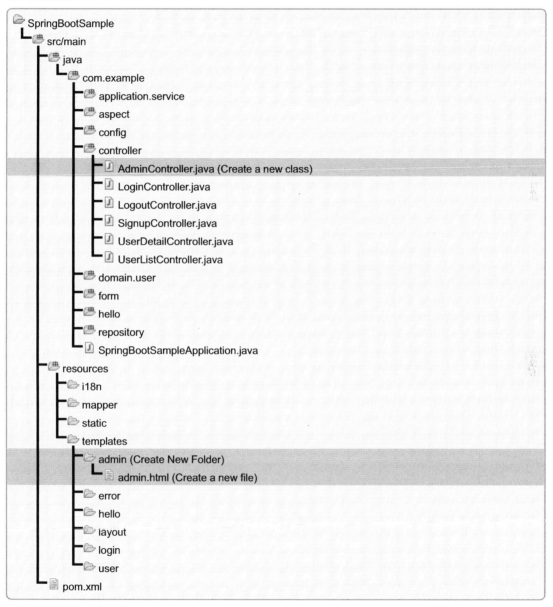

Source Code

First, create a screen dedicated to admin authority.
[admin.html]

```
<!DOCTYPE html>
<html xmlns:th="http://www.thymeleaf.org"
 xmlns:layout="http://www.ultraq.net.nz/thymeleaf/layout"
 layout:decorate="~{layout/layout}">
<head>
 <title>Admin authority only</title>
</head>
<body>
 <div layout:fragment="content">
  <div class="header border-bottom mt-2">
   <h1 class="h2">Admin authority only screen</h1>
  </div>
 </div>
</body>
</html>
```

Next, create a controller for the admin authority only screen.
[AdminController.java]

```
package com.example.controller;

import org.springframework.stereotype.Controller;
import org.springframework.web.bind.annotation.GetMapping;

@Controller
public class AdminController {

  /** Transition to the admin authority only screen */
  @GetMapping("/admin")
  public String getAdmin() {
    return "admin/admin";
  }
}
```

Add a link to the menu screen. The part where the background color is changed is the modified part.
[menu.html]

```
<!DOCTYPE html>
<html xmlns:th="http://www.thymeleaf.org"
 xmlns:layout="http://www.ultraq.net.nz/thymeleaf/layout"
 layout:decorate="~{layout/layout}">
<head>
</head>
```

```
<body>
 <div layout:fragment="menu" class="bg-light">
  <ul class="nav nav-pills nav-stacked flex-column">
   <li role="presentation">
    <a class="nav-link" th:href="@{'/user/list'}">User list</a>
   </li>
   <li role="presentation">
    <a class="nav-link" th:href="@{'/admin'}">Admin only</a>
   </li>
  </ul>
 </div>
</body>
</html>
```

Modify the security settings class. The part where the background color is changed is the modified part.

[SecurityConfig.java]

```
@EnableWebSecurity
@Configuration
public class SecurityConfig extends WebSecurityConfigurerAdapter {

  @Autowired
  private UserDetailsService userDetailsService;

  @Bean
  public PasswordEncoder passwordEncoder() {
    return new BCryptPasswordEncoder();
  }

  /** Set a target out-of-security */
  @Override
  public void configure(WebSecurity web) throws Exception {
    …(Omitted)
  }

  /** Various security settings */
  @Override
  protected void configure(HttpSecurity http) throws Exception {
    // Set of login unnecessary page
    http
      .authorizeRequests()
        .antMatchers("/login").permitAll() //Direct link OK
        .antMatchers("/user/signup").permitAll() //Direct link OK
        .antMatchers("/admin").hasAuthority("ROLE_ADMIN") // Authority control
        .anyRequest().authenticated(); // Otherwise direct link NG

    // Login process
    http
      .formLogin()
```

```
            .loginProcessingUrl("/login") // Login process path
            .loginPage("/login") // Specify login page
            .failureUrl("/login?error") // Transition destination when login fails
            .usernameParameter("userId") // Login page user ID
            .passwordParameter("password") // Login page password
            .defaultSuccessUrl("/user/list", true); // Transition destination after success

    // Logout process
    http
        .logout()
            .logoutRequestMatcher(new AntPathRequestMatcher("/logout"))
            .logoutUrl("/logout")
            .logoutSuccessUrl("/login?logout");

    // Disable CSRF measures (temporary)
    // http.csrf().disable();
    }

    /** Authentication settings */
    @Override
    protected void configure(AuthenticationManagerBuilder auth) throws Exception {
        ...(Omitted)
    }
}
```

Point: URL authorization

To set authorization for a given URL, use a method such as hasAuthority. Specify permissions for this method. If the user has that permission, they can access the URL.

Execution

Run SpringBoot and access the admin authority only screen from the user list screen. The execution result differs depending on which user logs in.

[User data]

User ID	Password	Authority
system@co.jp	password	Admin
user@co.jp	password	General

[Admin authority only screen] (Accessed by admin authority user)

SpringSample

User list

Admin only

Admin authority only screen

[Common error screen] (Access as a general authority user)

403 Forbidden

Access Denied

Please return to the login screen

Return to login screen

If you try to access it as a general authority user, you will get an HTTP 403 error. Therefore, the common error screen is displayed.

11.3.2 Screen display authorization

Overview

Depending on the user's privileges, it is possible to hide the item on the screen.

【General user】 　　　　【Admin user】

General user: SpringSample — User list — User List

Admin user: SpringSample — User list — Admin only — User List

Directory

There is no change in the directory structure.

Source Code

Modify the HTML of the menu screen.

[menu.html]

```
<!DOCTYPE html>
<html xmlns:th="http://www.thymeleaf.org"
  xmlns:layout="http://www.ultraq.net.nz/thymeleaf/layout"
  layout:decorate="~{layout/layout}"
  xmlns:sec="http://www.thymeleaf.org/extras/spring-security">
<head>
</head>
<body>
 <div layout:fragment="menu" class="bg-light">
  <ul class="nav nav-pills nav-stacked">
   <li role="presentation">
    <a class="nav-link" th:href="@{'/user/list'}">User list</a>
   </li>
   <li role="presentation" sec:authorize="hasRole('ADMIN')">
    <a class="nav-link" th:href="@{'/admin'}">Admin only</a>
   </li>
  </ul>
 </div>
</body>
</html>
```

Point: "sec:authorize" attribute

Use the sec: authorize attribute to decide whether to display the item on the screen by authority. Call the hasRole and hasAuthority methods within this attribute. Set roles for those methods. If the logged-in user has that role, the item will be displayed.

In addition, in order to use the "sec:authorize" attribute, it is necessary to add [xmlns:sec="http://www.thymeleaf.org/extras/spring-security"] to the html tag.

Note: Role name

When specifying a role in the authorization method, there are methods that must be prefixed with "ROLE_" and methods that omit "ROLE_".

[Example of specifying ROLE_ADMIN]

Method	Example
hasRole	hasRole("ADMIN")
hasAuthority	hasAuthority("ROLE_ADMIN")

Since the method of specifying the role differs depending on the method, it is better to unify the method to be used. Also, it's a good idea to always prefix the role name with "ROLE_".

Execution

Run SpringBoot and access the user list screen. The execution result differs depending on which user logs in.

[User data]

User ID	Password	Authority
system@co.jp	password	Admin
user@co.jp	password	General

【General user】

SpringSample

User list   User List

【Admin user】

SpringSample

User list   User List
Admin only

You could set whether to display the item by user authority.

Summary

Here's what you've learned in this chapter:

[Authentication]

- Disable security for access to static resources such as CSS.
- To allow a direct link, to set the [antMatchers("path").permitAll()].
- To prohibit direct links, set [anyRequest().authenticated()].
- With in-memory authentication, you can log in as a temporary user.
- To authenticate with user data, prepare a class that implements UserDetailsService.
- The password must be encrypted and registered.
- The error message at login is defined in messages.properties.
- To enable CSRF measures, use the "th:action" attribute in the form tag.

[Authorization]

- Authorization includes URL authorization and screen display authorization.
- URL of the authorization in the Security Settings, set the [antMatchers("path").hasAuthority("roll")].
- To authorize the screen display, add [sec:authorize="hasRole('roll')"] to the html tag.
- By the method of authorization, specifying role names are different.

12. REST

In this chapter you will learn about REST.

- REST overview
- REST implementation

12.1 REST overview

First, I'll explain what REST is.

- What is REST?
- Why use REST?

12.1.1 What is REST?

To briefly explain REST, it is a mechanism for using various Web services by sending HTTP requests. Normally, when you send an HTTP request, HTML is returned as a response.

[Normal HTTP request]

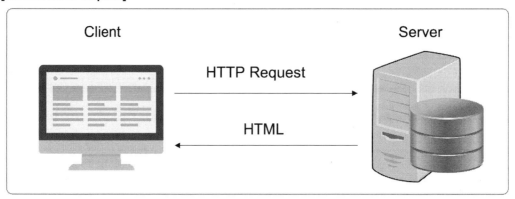

The browser interprets the HTML of the response and displays the result as a screen.

However, when you send a request with REST, the execution result of the Web service is returned. Web services are services such as weather and map information, or AI.

[REST execution image]

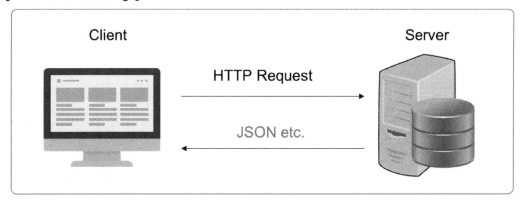

The application can interpret the REST response result and provide it to the user in various ways.

Therefore, the application can use the external Web service. If you use an existing service, you can simplify the part you prepare yourself, which will improve development efficiency. And in REST, it is mainstream to return the response in JSON format.

Note : What is JSON?

JSON is the format for describing objects in JavaScript. It stands for JavaScript Object Notation. It is a popular data format in REST because it has less data and is easier to read than XML.

In REST, the method of HTTP request is changed depending on what kind of operation is performed.

Operation	HTTP method
Search	GET
Registration	POST
Update	PUT
Delete	DELETE

You will use these methods in a sample you will create later.

12.1.2 Why use REST?

Modify the application you have created so far to use REST. To communicate via REST, make a request using JavaScript.

The reason for doing this is that it has the following merits.

[Merits of using REST]

- Increased processing speed by reducing communication volume
- Improved user operability

Increased processing speed by reducing communication volume

If you don't use REST, you'll get HTML every time you request. But with REST, you can receive only the results you need. The following is an explanation using a search example.

Without REST	Get all of the HTML every time you search. Renders the entire screen.
Using REST	Get only the search results in JSON. Renders only the search result part.

What is rendering?

Rendering is the screen drawing process.

Overall performance will improve if you use REST.

Improved user operability

The applications you have created so far are validated on the user signup screen. Press the "signup" button many times without entering anything, and then press the browser's back button. Then you will see the previous validation results instead of the login screen. Since the screen transition occurs every time the button is pressed, the behavior will be strange.

If you want to return to the login screen, you need to press the browser's back button as many times as you press the "signup" button. If you use REST, no screen transition will occur when the validation result is reflected on the screen. Therefore, you can also return to the login screen by pressing the back button on your browser.

With REST, you can do many other things. As a result, user operability is improved.

12.2 REST implementation

Now, let's add REST communication processing to the applications you have created so far.

- Update / Delete
- Registration / Validation
- Search

12.2.1 Update / Delete

Overview

First, let's create updates and deletes with REST. Create a button for REST on the user details screen.

[User details screen]

After updating or deleting with REST, redirect to the user list screen.

Directory

The directory structure is as follows. The part where the background color is changed is the new part to be added.

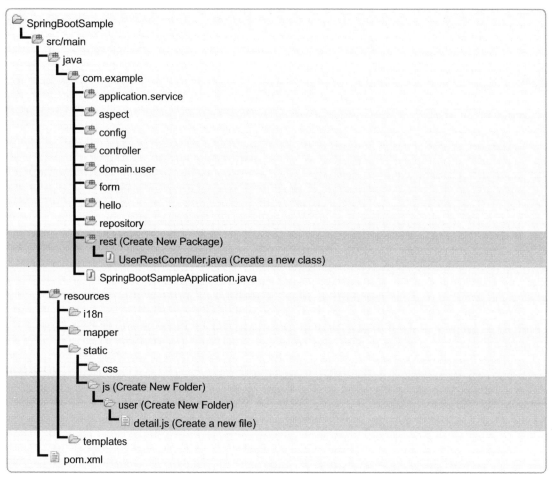

Source Code

First, create a controller for REST.

[UserRestController.java]

```
package com.example.rest;

import org.springframework.beans.factory.annotation.Autowired;
import org.springframework.web.bind.annotation.DeleteMapping;
import org.springframework.web.bind.annotation.PostMapping;
import org.springframework.web.bind.annotation.PutMapping;
```

```java
import org.springframework.web.bind.annotation.RequestBody;
import org.springframework.web.bind.annotation.RequestMapping;
import org.springframework.web.bind.annotation.RestController;

import com.example.domain.user.service.UserService;
import com.example.form.UserDetailForm;

@RestController
@RequestMapping("/user")
public class UserRestController {

    @Autowired
    private UserService userService;

    /** Update user */
    @PutMapping("/update")
    public int updateUser(UserDetailForm form) {
        // Update user
        userService.updateUserOne(form.getUserId(),
                form.getPassword(),
                form.getUserName());

        return 0;
    }

    /** Delete user */
    @DeleteMapping("/delete")
    public int deleteUser(UserDetailForm form) {
        // Delete user
        userService.deleteUserOne(form.getUserId());

        return 0;
    }
}
```

Point: @RestController

Annotate the class with @RestController. Then you can receive the return value of the method in that class in REST. To be precise, the return value of the method is returned as the HTTP response body.

In the sample code, users are updated and deleted using the services you have created so far.

Next, create the JavaScript for the user details screen. This JavaScript uses jQuery.
[detail.js]

```javascript
'use strict';

/** Processing when loading the screen */
jQuery(function($){
```

```javascript
    /** Update button processing */
    $('#btn-update').click(function (event) {
        // User update
        updateUser();
    });

    /** Delete button processing */
    $('#btn-delete').click(function (event) {
        // User delete
        deleteUser();
    });
});

/** User update processing */
function updateUser() {

    // Get the value of the form
    var formData = $('#user-detail-form').serializeArray();

    // ajax communication
    $.ajax({
        type : "PUT",
        cache : false,
        url : '/user/update',
        data: formData,
        dataType : 'json',
    }).done(function(data) {
        // ajax success
        alert('Updated user');
        // Redirect to user list screen
        window.location.href = '/user/list';

    }).fail(function(jqXHR, textStatus, errorThrown) {
        // ajax failed
        alert('Failed to update user');
    }).always(function() {
        // Process to always execute
    });
}

/** User delete processing */
function deleteUser() {

    // Get the value of the form
    var formData = $('#user-detail-form').serializeArray();

    // ajax communication
    $.ajax({
        type : "DELETE",
        cache : false,
```

```
        url : '/user/delete',
        data: formData,
        dataType : 'json',
    }).done(function(data) {
        // ajax success
        alert('Deleted user');
        // Redirect to user list screen
        window.location.href = '/user/list';

    }).fail(function(jqXHR, textStatus, errorThrown) {
        // ajax failed
        alert('Failed to delete user');

    }).always(function() {
        // Process to always execute
    });
}
```

Note: ajax communication

With jQuery, you can use the $.ajax function for ajax communication. Ajax communication is asynchronous communication. Asynchronous communication is a communication method that does not wait for server processing.

For example, request a time-consuming process from the server (such as a file download). Asynchronous communication allows the user to interact with the screen during that time.

In the sample code of this document, the following process is not performed after ajax communication, so it is redirected.

On the other hand, the synchronous communication is a communication method that the client waits until the server to complete processing. All requests using the form tags that have been created so far are in synchronous communication.

Attention: CSRF token

If you are taking CSRF measures with Spring Security, you need to send the CSRF token also in ajax communication. If you don't send the token, the communication will be repelled by security. In the sample code, the entire contents of the form are sent, so the CSRF token is included in the sent contents.

Finally, modify the user details screen.

[detail.html]

```
<!DOCTYPE html>
<html xmlns:th="http://www.thymeleaf.org"
```

```html
 xmlns:layout="http://www.ultraq.net.nz/thymeleaf/layout"
 layout:decorate="~{layout/layout}">
<head>
 <title>User Details</title>
 <!-- Read CSS -->
 <link rel="stylesheet" th:href="@{/css/user/list.css}">
 <!-- Read JS -->
 <script th:src="@{/js/user/detail.js}" defer></script>
</head>
<body>
 <div layout:fragment="content">
  <div class="header border-bottom">
   <h1 class="h2">User Details</h1>
  </div>
  <form id="user-detail-form" method="post" th:action="@{/user/detail}"
    class="form-signup" th:object="${userDetailForm}">
   <input type="hidden" th:field="*{userId}" />
   <!-- User Details information -->
   <table class="table table-striped table-bordered table-hover">
    ...(Omitted)
   </table>
   <!-- Button area -->
   <div class="text-center">
    <!-- Delete button -->
    <button class="btn btn-danger" type="submit" name="delete">
     delete
    </button>
    <!-- Update button -->
    <button class="btn btn-primary" type="submit" name="update">
     update
    </button>
   </div>
   <!-- REST button area -->
   <div class="text-center mt-2">
    <!-- Delete button -->
    <button id="btn-delete" class="btn btn-danger" type="button">
     delete(REST)
    </button>
    <!-- Update button -->
    <button id="btn-update" class="btn btn-primary" type="button">
     update(REST)
    </button>
   </div>
   <!-- Salary information -->
   <th:block th:if="*{salaryList != null and salaryList.size() > 0}">
    ...(Omitted)
   </th:block>
  </form>
 </div>
</body>
</html>
```

Execution

Run SpringBoot and access the user details screen.

[User details screen]

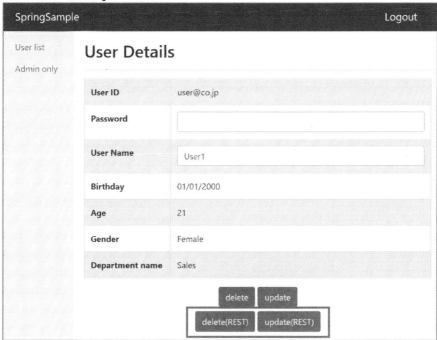

If the update or deletion is successful, the following message will be displayed.

[Success message]

When you press the "OK" button, you will be redirected to the user list screen. This completes the creation of the update and delete process using REST.

Note: Reaction

When making a screen, please add a reaction. Showing whether an operation succeeded or failed is one of the reactions.

Preparing the reaction is the basis of screen implementation.

In addition, it is common to display a confirmation message when you press the register / update / delete button. (Although not made in the sample of this book).

12.2.2 Registration / Validation

Overview

Next, create a registration and validation process in REST. Modify the user signup screen.

Directory

The directory structure is as follows. The part where the background color is changed is the new part to be added.

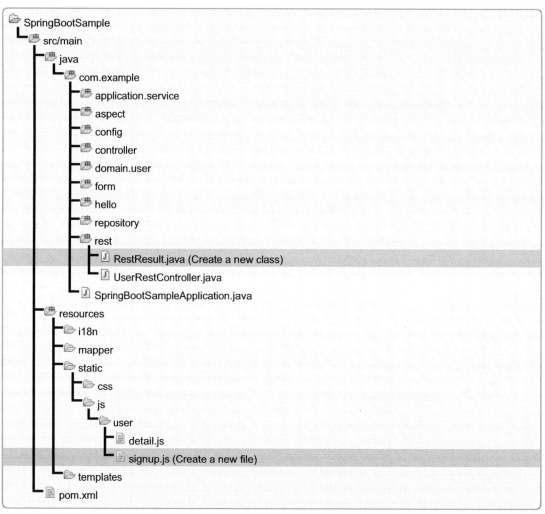

```
SpringBootSample
  src/main
    java
      com.example
        application.service
        aspect
        config
        controller
        domain.user
        form
        hello
        repository
        rest
          RestResult.java (Create a new class)
          UserRestController.java
        SpringBootSampleApplication.java
    resources
      i18n
      mapper
      static
        css
        js
          user
            detail.js
            signup.js (Create a new file)
      templates
    pom.xml
```

Source Code

First, modify the security setting class. The part where the background color is changed is the modified part.

[SecurityConfig.java]

```java
@EnableWebSecurity
@Configuration
public class SecurityConfig extends WebSecurityConfigurerAdapter {

    @Autowired
    private UserDetailsService userDetailsService;

    @Bean
    public PasswordEncoder passwordEncoder() {
        return new BCryptPasswordEncoder();
    }

    /** Set a target out-of-security */
    @Override
    public void configure(WebSecurity web) throws Exception {
        …(Omitted)
    }

    /** Various security settings */
    @Override
    protected void configure(HttpSecurity http) throws Exception {
        // Set of login unnecessary page
        http
            .authorizeRequests()
                .antMatchers("/login").permitAll() //Direct link OK
                .antMatchers("/user/signup").permitAll() //Direct link OK
                .antMatchers("/user/signup/rest").permitAll() //Direct link OK
                .antMatchers("/admin").hasAuthority("ROLE_ADMIN") // Authority control
                .anyRequest().authenticated(); // Otherwise direct link NG

        // Login process
        http
            .formLogin()
                .loginProcessingUrl("/login") // Login process path
                .loginPage("/login") // Specify login page
                .failureUrl("/login?error") // Transition destination when login fails
                .usernameParameter("userId") // Login page user ID
                .passwordParameter("password") // Login page password
                .defaultSuccessUrl("/user/list", true); // Transition destination after success

        // Logout process
        http
            .logout()
                .logoutRequestMatcher(new AntPathRequestMatcher("/logout"))
```

```
            .logoutUrl("/logout")
            .logoutSuccessUrl("/login?logout");

    // Disable CSRF measures (temporary)
    // http.csrf().disable();
  }

  /** Authentication settings */
  @Override
  protected void configure(AuthenticationManagerBuilder auth) throws Exception {
      …(Omitted)
  }
}
```

Updating and deleting users is a function used after user authentication. Therefore, it is not necessary to set direct link permission in the request destination URL. However, user registration is a process that anyone can do before logging in. Therefore, you need to allow direct links to the REST request URL.

Next, create the class returned by REST.
[RestResult.java]

```
package com.example.rest;

import java.util.Map;

import lombok.AllArgsConstructor;
import lombok.Data;

@Data
@AllArgsConstructor
public class RestResult {

  /** Return code */
  private int result;

  /** Error map
   * key: field name
   * value: error message
   */
  private Map<String, String> errors;
}
```

In the return code, enter the code value of whether or not it ended normally. In the errors field, enter the field name and error message for which the validation result was NG.

Next, modify the controller for REST. The part where the background color is changed is the modified part.

[UserRestController.java]

```
package com.example.rest;

import java.util.HashMap;
import java.util.Locale;
import java.util.Map;

import org.modelmapper.ModelMapper;
import org.springframework.beans.factory.annotation.Autowired;
import org.springframework.context.MessageSource;
import org.springframework.validation.BindingResult;
import org.springframework.validation.FieldError;
import org.springframework.validation.annotation.Validated;
import org.springframework.web.bind.annotation.DeleteMapping;
import org.springframework.web.bind.annotation.PostMapping;
import org.springframework.web.bind.annotation.PutMapping;
import org.springframework.web.bind.annotation.RequestMapping;
import org.springframework.web.bind.annotation.RestController;

import com.example.domain.user.model.User;
import com.example.domain.user.service.UserService;
import com.example.form.GroupOrder;
import com.example.form.SignupForm;
import com.example.form.UserDetailForm;

@RestController
@RequestMapping("/user")
public class UserRestController {

    @Autowired
    private UserService userService;

    @Autowired
    private ModelMapper modelMapper;

    @Autowired
    private MessageSource messageSource;

    /** User signup */
    @PostMapping("/signup/rest")
    public RestResult postSignup(@Validated(GroupOrder.class) SignupForm form,
        BindingResult bindingResult, Locale locale) {

      // Input check result
      if (bindingResult.hasErrors()) {
        // Check result: NG
        Map<String, String> errors = new HashMap<>();

        // Get error message
```

283

```
        for (FieldError error : bindingResult.getFieldErrors()) {
            String message = messageSource.getMessage(error, locale);
            errors.put(error.getField(), message);
        }
        // Return error result
        return new RestResult(90, errors);
    }

    // Convert form to MUser class
    MUser user = modelMapper.map(form, MUser.class);

    // user signup
    userService.signup(user);

    // Return result
    return new RestResult(0, null);
}

/** Update user */
@PutMapping("/update")
public int updateUser(UserDetailForm form) {
    ...(Omitted)
}

/** Delete user */
@DeleteMapping("/delete")
public int deleteUser(UserDetailForm form) {
    ...(Omitted)
}
}
```

Point 1: FieldError

The name of the field whose validation result is NG can be obtained from the FieldError class. However, only fields whose single item check result is NG can be obtained from FieldError.

Not made in this book of the sample, but you can make your own validation. With your own validation, you can perform correlation checks that compare two fields at the same time. In such cases, the ObjectError class contains the validation result.

You can also get the error message by passing FieldError and Locale to MessageSource.

Point 2: Return value

In the controller for REST, set the return value of the method to Java class. Then the Java class will be automatically converted to JSON. JSON is set in the HTTP response.

The return code is set as follows.

Resutl	Return code
Successful completion	0
Validation result NG	90

Next, modify the user signup screen. The part where the background color is changed is the modified part.

[signup.html]

```
<!DOCTYPE html>
<html xmlns:th="http://www.thymeleaf.org">
<head>
 <meta charset="UTF-8"></meta>
 <meta name="viewport" content="width=device-width, initial-scale=1, shrink-to-fit=no">
 <!-- Read CSS -->
 <link rel="stylesheet" th:href="@{/webjars/bootstrap/css/bootstrap.min.css}">
 <link rel="stylesheet" th:href="@{/css/user/signup.css}">
 <!-- Read JS -->
 <script th:src="@{/webjars/jquery/jquery.min.js}" defer></script>
 <script th:src="@{/webjars/bootstrap/js/bootstrap.min.js}" defer></script>
 <script th:src="@{/js/user/signup.js}" defer></script>
 <title th:text="#{user.signup.title}"></title>
</head>
<body class="bg-light">
 <form id="signup-form" method="post" action="/user/signup"
   class="form-signup" th:object="${signupForm}">
  <h1 class="text-center" th:text="#{user.signup.title}"></h1>
  <!-- User ID -->
  <div class="form-group">
   ...(Omitted)
  </div>
  <!-- Password -->
  <div class="form-group" >
   ...(Omitted)
  </div>
  <!-- User Name -->
  <div class="form-group">
   ...(Omitted)
  </div>
  <!-- Birthday -->
  <div class="form-group">
   ...(Omitted)
  </div>
  <!-- Age -->
  <div class="form-group">
   ...(Omitted)
```

```
    </div>
    <!-- Gender -->
    <div class="form-group">
      ...(Omitted)
    <div>
    <!-- Signup button -->
    <input type="submit" th:value="#{user.signup.btn}"
      class="btn btn-primary w-100 mt-3" />
    <button id="btn-signup" type="button"
      class="btn btn-primary w-100 mt-3">
      signup(REST)
    </button>
    <input type="hidden" th:name="${_csrf.parameterName}"
        th:value="${_csrf.token}" />
  </form>
</body>
</html>
```

Finally, create the JavaScript for the user registration screen.

[signup.js]

```javascript
'use strict';

/** Processing when loading the screen */
jQuery(function($){

  /** Signup button processing */
  $('#btn-signup').click(function (event) {
    // user signup
    signupUser();
  });
});

/** User signup process */
function signupUser() {
  // Clear validation results
  removeValidResult();

  // Get the value of the form
  var formData = $('#signup-form').serializeArray();

  // ajax communication
  $.ajax({
    type : "POST",
    cache : false,
    url : '/user/signup/rest',
    data: formData,
    dataType : 'json',
  }).done(function(data) {
    // ajax success
```

```
      console.log(data);

    if (data.result === 90) {
      // When a validation error occurs
      $.each(data.errors, function (key, value) {
        reflectValidResult(key, value)
      });

    } else if (data.result === 0) {
      alert('Signed up user');
      // Redirect to login screen
      window.location.href = '/login';
    }

  }).fail(function(jqXHR, textStatus, errorThrown) {
    // ajax failed
    alert('User signup failed');

  }).always(function() {
    // Process to always execute
  });
}

/** Clear validation results */
function removeValidResult() {
  $('.is-invalid').removeClass('is-invalid');
  $('.invalid-feedback').remove();
  $('.text-danger').remove();
}

/** Reflection of the validation result */
function reflectValidResult(key, value) {
  // Add error message
  if (key === 'gender') { // For gender fields
    // Apply CSS
    $('input[name=' + key + ']').addClass('is-invalid');
    // Add error message
    $('input[name=' + key + ']')
      .parent().parent()
      .append('<div class="text-danger">' + value + '</div>');

  } else { // For fields other than gender
    // Apply CSS
    $('input[id=' + key + ']').addClass('is-invalid');
    // Add error message
    $('input[id=' + key + ']')
      .after('<div class="invalid-feedback">' + value + '</div>');
  }
}
```

When you press the REST signup button, the following processing will be performed.

1. Clearing validation results
2. user registration
3. If the validation result is NG, an error message is displayed.
4. If successful, redirect to the login screen

Note1: Get execution result

After the ajax communication is successful with jQuery, the processing inside the "done" function is performed. In the "done" function, the JSON of the execution result is put in the data variable. In the sample of this book, the value of RestResult converted to JSON is included.

The contents of the data variable are output to the log in the following part.

```
console.log(data);
```

Use "console.log" only when debugging. When actually creating an application, use the debug function of your browser.

Note: $.each

You can iterate using jQuery's $ .each function. The first argument of this function is the object to be iteratively processed. The sample code in this book is as follows.

```
$.each(data.errors, function (key, value) {
```

"data.errors" refers to the value in the "errors" field of RestResult. The "errors" field is of type Map with key and value. Therefore, in the [function(key, value)] part of the second argument, the key and value in the "errors" field are extracted.

Execution

Run SpringBoot and access the user signup screen. Press the "signup(REST)" button without entering anything.

[Execution result]

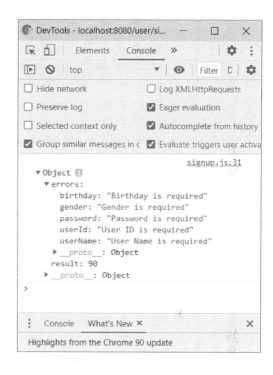

The validation result is reflected on the screen. If you press the "F12" key at this time, the developer screen will be displayed. The log is output to the "Console" tab. The RestResult class specified in "console.log" is output.

12.2.3 Search

Overview

Perform user search with REST and list the results. Add a button and a display area for search results as shown below.

[User list screen]

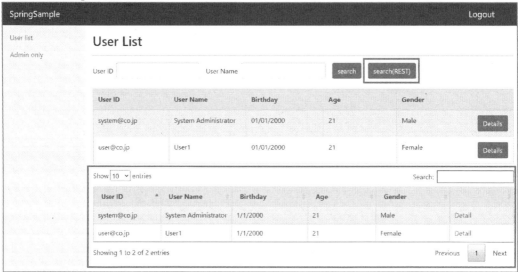

Use the DataTables library to display search results. DataTables uses jQuery internally. It is very difficult to reflect the JSON of the search results on the screen. However, if you use the library, you can easily display it on the screen.

Directory

The directory structure is as follows. The part where the background color is changed is the new part to be added.

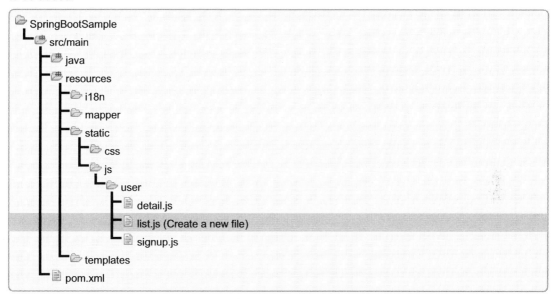

Source Code

First, add the DataTables library in webjars. Add the following code inside the dependencies tag of pom.xml. The part where the background color is changed is the added part.

[pom.xml]

```xml
<dependencies>
  ...
  <!-- datatables -->
  <dependency>
    <groupId>org.webjars</groupId>
    <artifactId>datatables</artifactId>
    <version>1.10.21</version>
  </dependency>
  <!-- datatables-plugins -->
  <dependency>
    <groupId>org.webjars</groupId>
    <artifactId>datatables-plugins</artifactId>
    <version>1.10.21</version>
    <scope>runtime</scope>
  </dependency>
  ...
</dependencies>
```

Next, modify the controller for REST. The part where the background color is changed is the modified part.

[UserRestController.java]

```java
@RestController
@RequestMapping("/user")
public class UserRestController {

    @Autowired
    private UserService userService;

    @Autowired
    private ModelMapper modelMapper;

    @Autowired
    private MessageSource messageSource;

    /** User search */
    @GetMapping("/get/list")
    public List<MUser> getUserList(UserListForm form) {

        // Convert form to MUser class
        MUser user = modelMapper.map(form, MUser.class);

        // Get user list
        List<MUser> userList = userService.getUsers(user);
        return userList;
    }

    /** User signup */
    @PostMapping("/signup/rest")
    public RestResult postSignup(@Validated(GroupOrder.class) SignupForm form,
        BindingResult bindingResult, Locale locale) {
        …(Omitted)
    }

    /** Update user */
    @PutMapping("/update")
    public int updateUser(UserDetailForm form) {
        …(Omitted)
    }

    /** Delete user */
    @DeleteMapping("/delete")
    public int deleteUser(UserDetailForm form) {
        …(Omitted)
    }
}
```

List<MUser> is the return value. List<MUser> is also converted to JSON.

Next, modify the user list screen. The part where the background color is changed is the modified part.

[list.html]

```html
<!DOCTYPE html>
<html xmlns:th="http://www.thymeleaf.org"
  xmlns:layout="http://www.ultraq.net.nz/thymeleaf/layout"
  layout:decorate="~{layout/layout}">
<head>
 <title>User List</title>
 <!-- Read Dedicated CSS -->
 <link rel="stylesheet" th:href="@{/css/user/list.css}">
 <!-- Read JS -->
 <link rel="stylesheet" th:href="@{/webjars/datatables/css/jquery.dataTables.min.css}">
 <script th:src="@{/webjars/datatables/js/jquery.dataTables.min.js}" defer></script>
 <script th:src="@{/js/user/list.js}" defer></script>
</head>
<body>
 <div layout:fragment="content">
  <div class="header border-bottom">
   <h1 class="h2">User List</h1>
  </div>
  <!-- Search -->
  <div class="mb-4">
   <form id="user-search-form" method="post" th:action="@{/user/list}"
     class="form-inline" th:object="${userListForm}">
    <div class="form-group" >
     <label for="userId" class="mr-2">User ID</label>
     <input type="text" class="form-control" th:field="*{userId}"/>
    </div>
    <div class="form-group mx-sm-3" >
     <label for="userName" class="mr-2">User Name</label>
     <input type="text" class="form-control" th:field="*{userName}"/>
    </div>
    <button class="btn btn-primary" type="submit">
    search
    </button>
    <button id="btn-search" class="btn btn-primary ml-3" type="button">
    search(REST)
    </button>
   </form>
  </div>
  <!-- List display -->
  <div>
   <table class="table table-striped table-bordered table-hover">
    …(Omitted)
   </table>
  </div>
  <!-- List display(REST) -->
  <div>
   <table id="user-list-table"
     class="table table-striped table-bordered table-hover w-100">
    <thead class="thead-light">
```

```
      <tr>
        <th class="th-width">User ID</th>
        <th class="th-width">User Name</th>
        <th class="th-width">Birthday</th>
        <th class="th-width">Age</th>
        <th class="th-width">Gender</th>
        <th class="th-width"></th>
      </tr>
    </thead>
  </table>
  </div>
  </div>
</body>
</html>
```

DataTables makes it easy to reflect JSON in HTML table tags.

Finally, create the JavaScript for the user list screen.

[list.js]

```
'use strict';

var userData = null;
var table = null; // DataTables object

/** Processing when loading the screen */
jQuery(function($){

  // DataTables initialization
  createDataTables();

  /** Search button processing */
  $('#btn-search').click(function (event) {
    // Search
    search();
  });
});

/** Search processing */
function search() {

  // Get the value of form
  var formData = $('#user-search-form').serialize();

  // ajax communication
  $.ajax({
    type : "GET",
    url : '/user/get/list',
    data: formData,
    dataType : 'json',
    contentType: 'application/json; charset=UTF-8',
```

```
      cache : false,
      timeout : 5000,
  }).done(function(data) {
      // ajax success
      console.log(data);
      // Put JSON to variable
      userData = data;
      // Create DataTables
      createDataTables();

  }).fail(function(jqXHR, textStatus, errorThrown) {
      // ajax failed
      alert('Search process failed');

  }).always(function() {
      // Process to always execute
  });
}

/** Create DataTables */
function createDataTables() {

  // If DataTables has already been created
  if (table !== null) {
      // DataTables discard
      table.destroy();
  }

  // Create DataTables
  table = $('#user-list-table').DataTable({
      //Display data
      data: userData,
      //Data and column mapping
      columns: [
        { data: 'userId'},
        { data: 'userName'},
        {
           data: 'birthday',
           render: function ( data, type, row ) {
             var date = new Date(data);
             var year = date.getFullYear();
             var month = date.getMonth() + 1;
             var date = date.getDate();
             return date + '/' + month + '/' + year;
           }
        },
        { data: 'age'},
        {
           data: 'gender',
           render: function ( data, type, row ) {
             var gender = '';
```

```
          if (data === 1) {
              gender = 'Male';
          } else {
              gender = 'Female';
          }
          return gender;
        }
    },
    {
        data: 'userId', // URL of user details screen
        render: function ( data, type, row ) {
            var url = '<a href="/user/detail/' + data + '">Detail</a>';
            return url;
        }
    },
  ]
});
}
```

Note: How to use DataTables

When I explain how to use DataTables, I run out of pages. Therefore, I will explain it briefly.

The first is to pass the JSON of the search results to DataTables. It passes a variable with JSON in the "data" attribute. In the sample code, JSON is passed to the "data" attribute in the following part.

```
//Display data
data: userData,
```

Next, specify which JSON data is displayed in which column of the table with the "columns" attribute. In the sample code, the table column and JSON are mapped in the following part.

```
columns: [
    { data: 'userId'},
    { data: 'userName'},
    ...
```

It is displayed in the HTML table in the order specified in the "columns" attribute. Therefore, in the sample code above, the user ID is displayed in the first column and the user name is displayed in the second column. To display which data in JSON, specify the key name in JSON.

Also, if you want to convert the value and display it, specify the "render" attribute. In the sample code, the display contents are changed according to the gender value in the following part.

```
{
    data: 'gender',
    render: function ( data, type, row ) {
```

```
    var gender = ";
    if (data === 1) {
        gender = 'Male';
    } else {
        gender = 'Female';
    }
    return gender;
    }
},
```

Execution

Run SpringBoot and access the user list screen.

[User list screen]

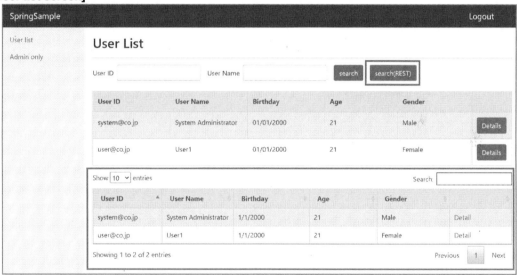

Press the "Search (REST)" button to display the search results.

After searching, press F12 to open the developer screen. When you press the "Console" tab, the JSON of List <MUser> will be displayed as shown below.

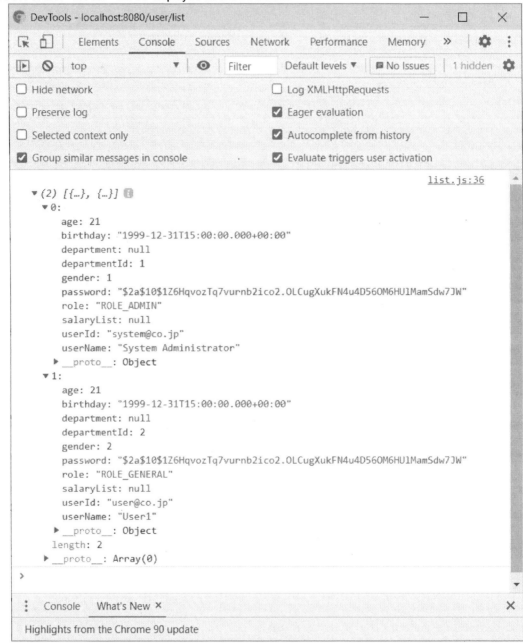

Summary

Here's what you've learned in this chapter.

[REST Overview]

- REST allows you to use external web services.
- Using REST has the following advantages.

    - Increased processing speed by reducing communication volume
    - Improved user operability

[REST implementation]

- Annotate the controller for REST with @RestController.
- If CSRF measures are enabled, send a CSRF token.
- In jQuery, to request using the "$.ajax" function.

13. Spring Data JPA

In this chapter you will learn how to use JPA with Spring.

- Overview
- Basic
- Advanced

13.1 Overview

JPA is a Java standard O/R mapper. If it is simple SQL, JPA will generate it automatically. Therefore, development efficiency can be improved. JPA is an abbreviation for Java Persistence API.

However, if you try to use JPA as it is, there are some troublesome parts. However, if you use Spring Data JPA, you can use JPA without considering the troublesome part.

Note: What is Spring Data?

The code you implement depends on which database product you use. Code will not change significantly between RDB products such as Oracle and PostgreSQL. However, the code is very different between RDB and NoSQL. NoSQL is a database that has a completely different structure from relational databases.

Spring Data is a library that eliminates differences such as RDB and NoSQL.

13.2 Basic

Now let's learn how to use JPA. First of all, you will learn from the basic usage.

- CRUD
- Arbitrary SQL

13.2.1 CRUD

Overview

First, learn CRUD operations using JPA. CRUD is an acronym for Create, Read, Update, and Delete. That is, SQL insert, select, update, delete.

The part that has access to the database with MyBatis until now, we will replaced by the JPA. Therefore, some functions can be used and some functions cannot be used temporarily. Eventually all functions will be available.

Of the functions created with MyBatis, you need to create the following functions.

Function	Correspondence
Regist user	✓
Get user(multiple)	✓
Get user(1record)	✓
Update user	-
Delete user	✓
Get login user	✓
Dynamic SQL generation (change search conditions)	-
Get department	-
Get salary list	-

In this section, you will create functions with a check mark for correspondence.

Directory

The directory structure is as follows. The part where the background color is changed is the new part to be added.

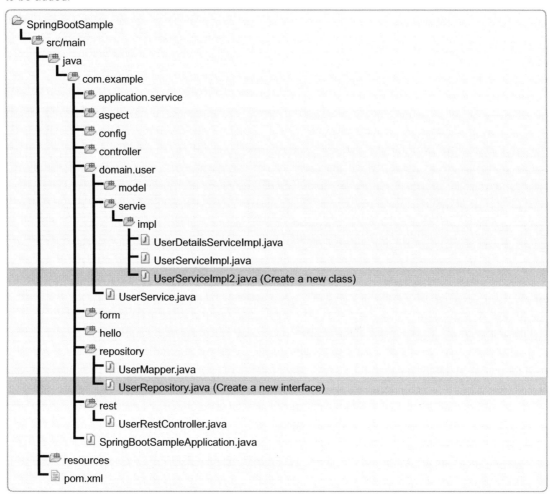

```
SpringBootSample
  src/main
    java
      com.example
        application.service
        aspect
        config
        controller
        domain.user
          model
          servie
            impl
              UserDetailsServiceImpl.java
              UserServiceImpl.java
              UserServiceImpl2.java (Create a new class)
          UserService.java
        form
        hello
        repository
          UserMapper.java
          UserRepository.java (Create a new interface)
        rest
          UserRestController.java
        SpringBootSampleApplication.java
    resources
    pom.xml
```

Source Code

First, modify pom.xml to add the JPA library. Add the following code inside the dependencies tag of pom.xml. The part where the background color is changed is the added part.

[pom.xml]

```
<dependencies>
  ...
  <!-- JPA -->
  <dependency>
    <groupId>org.springframework.boot</groupId>
    <artifactId>spring-boot-starter-data-jpa</artifactId>
  </dependency>
  ...
</dependencies>
```

Next, add the JPA settings. The part where the background color is changed is the modified part.

[application.properties]

```
# DataSource
spring.datasource.url=jdbc:h2:mem:testdb;DB_CLOSE_DELAY=-1;DB_CLOSE_ON_EXIT=FALSE
spring.datasource.driver-class-name=org.h2.Driver
spring.datasouce.username=sa
spring.datasouce.password=
spring.datasource.sql-script-encoding=UTF-8
spring.datasource.initialize=true
spring.datasource.schema=classpath:schema.sql
spring.datasource.data=classpath:data.sql

# H2DB
spring.h2.console.enabled=true

# message
spring.messages.basename=i18n/messages,i18n/ValidationMessages

# MyBatis
mybatis.mapper-locations=classpath*:/mapper/h2/*.xml

# Log Level
logging.level.com.example=debug

# =================
# JPA
# =================
# Table automatic creation
spring.jpa.hibernate.ddl-auto=none
# Output SQL to log
logging.level.org.hibernate.SQL=debug
# Output bind parameters to log
```

```
logging.level.org.hibernate.type.descriptor.sql.BasicBinder=trace
logging.level.org.hibernate.type.EnumType=trace
```

Point: JPA settings

If you add @Entity annotation to Java class, JPA has a function to automatically generate a table. You can set whether to use the function with the "spring.jpa.hibernate.ddl-auto" property. The sample code will not use that feature.

Other properties are settings for outputting SQL and parameters executed by JPA to the log.

Next, prepare the JPA repository.

[UserRepository.java]

```
package com.example.repository;

import org.springframework.data.jpa.repository.JpaRepository;

import com.example.domain.user.model.MUser;

public interface UserRepository extends JpaRepository<MUser, String> {

}
```

Point: JpaRepository

When creating a repository with JPA, it inherits JpaRepository. Specify the following types for generics of JpaRepository.

[Jpa Repository Generics]

```
JpaRepository<Data model type, primary key type>
```

Also, when inheriting JpaRepository, @Repository annotation can be omitted.

Then modify the entity class in the user master. The part where the background color is changed is the modified part.

[MUser.java]

```
package com.example.domain.user.model;

import java.util.Date;
import java.util.List;

import javax.persistence.Entity;
import javax.persistence.Id;
```

```java
import javax.persistence.Table;
import javax.persistence.Transient;

import lombok.Data;

@Data
@Entity
@Table(name="m_user")
public class MUser {
    @Id
    private String userId;
    private String password;
    private String userName;
    private Date birthday;
    private Integer age;
    private Integer gender;
    private Integer departmentId;
    private String role;
    @Transient
    private Department department;
    @Transient
    private List<Salary> salaryList;
}
```

Point1: @Entity

Annotate the entity class with @Entity. This annotation maps the class to a table in the database. Also, a table with the same name as the class name will be created in the DB. (The feature is turned off in the settings)

Point2: @Table

JPA tries to map the data with the same table name as the class name. If the class name and table name are different, add the @Table annotation. Set the table name you want to map in the "name" attribute of this annotation.

Point3: @Id

Annotate the primary key field with @Id. By doing so, JPA will recognize that this field is the primary key.

Note: @Transient

Annotate the fields that you do not want to do O/R mapping with @Transient.

The department and salary fields are temporarily annotated with @Transient.

Next, create a new service using JPA.

[UserServiceImpl2.java]

```java
package com.example.domain.user.service.impl;

import java.util.List;
import java.util.Optional;

import org.springframework.beans.factory.annotation.Autowired;
import org.springframework.context.annotation.Primary;
import org.springframework.security.crypto.password.PasswordEncoder;
import org.springframework.stereotype.Service;

import com.example.domain.user.model.MUser;
import com.example.domain.user.service.UserService;
import com.example.repository.UserRepository;

@Service
@Primary
public class UserServiceImpl2 implements UserService {

    @Autowired
    private UserRepository repository;

    @Autowired
    private PasswordEncoder encoder;

    /** User signup */
    @Transactional
    @Override
    public void signup(MUser user) {
        // Existence check
        boolean exists = repository.existsById(user.getUserId());
        if (exists) {
            throw new DataAccessException("User already exists"){};
        }

        user.setDepartmentId(1);
        user.setRole("ROLE_GENERAL");

        // Password encryption
        String rawPassword = user.getPassword();
        user.setPassword(encoder.encode(rawPassword));

        // insert
        repository.save(user);
    }

    /** Get user */
    @Override
    public List<MUser> getUsers(MUser user) {
```

```
      return repository.findAll();
   }

   /** Get user(1record) */
   @Override
   public MUser getUserOne(String userId) {
      Optional<MUser> option = repository.findById(userId);
      MUser user = option.orElse(null);
      return user;
   }

   /** Update user */
   @Transactional
   @Override
   public void updateUserOne(String userId, String password, String userName) {

   }

   /** Delete user */
   @Transactional
   @Override
   public void deleteUserOne(String userId) {
      repository.deleteById(userId);
   }

   /** Get login user */
   @Override
   public MUser getLoginUser(String userId) {
      Optional<MUser> option = repository.findById(userId);
      MUser user = option.orElse(null);
      return user;
   }
}
```

Point1: @Primary

If you prepare multiple classes that implement the same interface, it will be difficult for Spring to determine which class to DI. In such cases, you need to specify which class to assign. There are multiple ways to specify the DI target.

One way to specify the DI target is to add the @Primary annotation to the class. With this annotation, the class will be prioritized for DI.

Point2: JPA CRUD

JpaRepository provides multiple methods by default. With those methods, you can create simple CRUD operations. The following methods are used in the sample code in this book.

Purpose of use	Method
Primary key search	findById(primary key)
Search all	findAll()
Registration / Update	save(Data model)
Delete 1 record	deleteById(primary key)

Among them, use the "save" method to register and update. If the same data as the primary key does not exist in the database, the registration process will be performed. If the same data as the primary key exists in the database, the update process will be performed. Therefore, in the sample code of this book, the registration process checks whether the data exists. Also, the update process has not been created yet. Create an update process with [13.2.2 Arbitrary SQL].

Execution

Run SpringBoot and check if the following functions can be used.

Function
Regist user
Get user(multiple)
Get user(1record)
Delete user
Get login user

In addition, the following functions are not available at this time.

- Search on the user list screen. (All users are displayed)
- The department and salary will not be displayed on the user details screen.
- Users cannot be updated on the user details screen.

Look at the logs to see if you're really switching to JPA.

[Log] (Excerpt)

Method start: MUser com.example.domain.user.service.impl.**UserServiceImpl2**.getLoginUser(String)

If UserServiceImpl2 is output as the execution class, it has been switched to JPA.

13.2.2 Arbitrary SQL

Overview

Here you will learn how to use arbitrary SQL.

Among the functions that must be replaced from MyBatis, the following functions remain.

Function	Correspondence
Update user	✓
Get login user	✓
Dynamic SQL generation (change search conditions)	-
Get department	-
Get salary list	-

In this section, you will create functions with a check mark for correspondence. The [Get Login User] function was created in the previous section. However, since it will affect the development function after this, we will remake the process.

Directory

There is no change in the directory structure.

Source Code

First, modify the JPA repository. The part where the background color is changed is the modified part.

[UserRepository.java]

```java
package com.example.repository;

import org.springframework.data.jpa.repository.JpaRepository;
import org.springframework.data.jpa.repository.Modifying;
import org.springframework.data.jpa.repository.Query;
import org.springframework.data.repository.query.Param;

import com.example.domain.user.model.MUser;

public interface UserRepository extends JpaRepository<MUser, String> {

    /** Login user search */
    @Query("select user"
        + " from MUser user"
        + " where userId = :userId")
    public MUser findLoginUser(@Param("userId") String userId);

    /** User update */
    @Modifying
    @Query("update MUser"
        + " set"
        + "   password = :password"
        + "   , userName = :userName"
        + " where"
        + "   userId = :userId")
    public Integer updateUser(@Param("userId") String userId,
        @Param("password") String password,
        @Param("userName") String userName);

}
```

Point1: @Query / @Param

If you prepare a method with @Query annotation, you can prepare a method that can execute arbitrary SQL. Write the SQL inside the @Query annotation.

However, this SQL does not use table or column names. Instead, use Java class names and field names. This is a query language called JPQL used by JPA. You can also write pure SQL by specifying true for the nativeQuery attribute.

Also, method arguments can be embedded in the query with ": variable name". You can use the @Param annotation to rename method arguments.

Point2: @Modifying

When executing insert / update / delete statements and DDL using @Query annotation, @Modifying annotation must be added.

Next, modify the service for JPA. The part where the background color is changed is the modified part.
[UserServiceImpl2.java]

```
@Service
@Primary
public class UserServiceImpl2 implements UserService {

    @Autowired
    private UserRepository repository;

    @Autowired
    private PasswordEncoder encoder;

    /** User signup */
    @Transactional
    @Override
    public void signup(MUser user) {
        ...(Omitted)
    }

    /** Get user */
    @Override
    public List<MUser> getUsers(MUser user) {
        return repository.findAll();
    }

    /** Get user(1record) */
    @Override
    public MUser getUserOne(String userId) {
        ...(Omitted)
    }

    /** Update user */
    @Transactional
    @Override
    public void updateUserOne(String userId, String password, String userName) {

        // Password encryption
        String encryptPassword = encoder.encode(password);

        // User update
        repository.updateUser(userId, encryptPassword, userName);
    }

    /** Delete user */
```

```
    @Transactional
    @Override
    public void deleteUserOne(String userId) {
        repository.deleteById(userId);
    }

    /** Get login user */
    @Override
    public MUser getLoginUser(String userId) {
        return repository.findLoginUser(userId);
    }
}
```

In order to execute a method with @Modifying annotation, it must be annotated with @Transactional. Regardless of the presence or absence of @Modifying annotation, you should put a @Transactional annotation if the SQL insert, update, and delete. (Until now, I didn't annotate @Transactional)

Execution

Run SpringBoot and access the user details screen. The display of the execution result is omitted, but the user can be updated.

Note: Automatic generation of select statement

It is also possible to automatically generate a select statement by preparing a method that follows a specific rule. For example, provide a method called findByUserName (String userName). Then, you can search by user name without preparing SQL. Besides, you can sort and so on.

13.3 Advanced

From here, you will learn the advanced version of JPA.

- Dynamic SQL
- Table join (many-to-one)
- Table join (one-to-many)

13.3.1 Dynamic SQL

Overview

Learn how to use dynamic SQL to change search criteria.

Among the functions that must be replaced from MyBatis, the following functions remain.

Function	Correspondence
Dynamic SQL generation (change search conditions)	✓
Get department	-
Get salary list	-

In this section, you will create functions with a check mark for correspondence.

Directory

There is no change in the directory structure.

Source Code

Modify the service for JPA. The part where the background color is changed is the modified part.

[UserServiceImpl2.java]

```java
package com.example.domain.user.service.impl;

import java.util.List;
import java.util.Optional;

import org.springframework.beans.factory.annotation.Autowired;
import org.springframework.context.annotation.Primary;
import org.springframework.data.domain.Example;
import org.springframework.data.domain.ExampleMatcher;
import org.springframework.data.domain.ExampleMatcher.StringMatcher;
import org.springframework.security.crypto.password.PasswordEncoder;
import org.springframework.stereotype.Service;

import com.example.domain.user.model.MUser;
import com.example.domain.user.service.UserService;
import com.example.repository.UserRepository;

@Service
@Primary
public class UserServiceImpl2 implements UserService {

    @Autowired
    private UserRepository repository;

    @Autowired
    private PasswordEncoder encoder;

    /** User signup */
    @Transactional
    @Override
    public void signup(MUser user) {
        ...(Omitted)
    }

    /** Get user */
    @Override
    public List<MUser> getUsers(MUser user) {

        // Search conditions
        ExampleMatcher matcher = ExampleMatcher
            .matching() // and condition
            .withStringMatcher(StringMatcher.CONTAINING) // Like clause
            .withIgnoreCase(); // Both uppercase and lowercase

        return repository.findAll(Example.of(user, matcher));
```

```
}

/** Get user(1record) */
@Override
public MUser getUserOne(String userId) {
    ...(Omitted)
}

/** Update user */
@Transactional
@Override
public void updateUserOne(String userId, String password, String userName) {
    ...(Omitted)
}

/** Delete user */
@Transactional
@Override
public void deleteUserOne(String userId) {
    repository.deleteById(userId);
}

/** Get login user */
@Override
public MUser getLoginUser(String userId) {
    return repository.findLoginUser(userId);
}
}
```

Point: Example and Example Matcher

To generate dynamic SQL and change the search criteria, use the "Example" class. You can change the search criteria by passing the "Example" class to the findAll method. If you pass the entity class to the "Example" class, the values in it will be used for the search. If you pass only the entity class to the "Example" class, the search condition will be "and condition" and "all matches".

Use ExampleMatcher to change the search criteria. Using ExampleMatcher, you can specify "and condition", "or condition", "LIKE search", etc.

Execution

You will be able to search for users on the user list screen. (The execution result is omitted).

13.3.2 Table join (many-to-one)

Overview

Learn how to join tables in JPA. How to make it depends on the multiplicity between the tables. Multiplicity is a one-to-many, one-to-one, etc. In this section, you will learn how to join tables in the case of many-to-one.

Among the functions that must be replaced from MyBatis, the following functions remain.

Function	Correspondence
Get department	✓
Get salary list	-

In this section, you will create functions with a check mark for correspondence.

Directory

There is no change in the directory structure.

Source Code

First, modify the entity class of the department. The part where the background color is changed is the modified part.

[Department.java]

```java
package com.example.domain.user.model;

import javax.persistence.Entity;
import javax.persistence.Id;
import javax.persistence.Table;

import lombok.Data;

@Data
@Entity
@Table(name="m_department")
public class Department {
    @Id
    private Integer departmentId;
    private String departmentName;
}
```

By annotating @Entity etc., JPA is made to recognize it as an entity class.

Then modify the entity class of user master table. The part where the background color is changed is the modified part.

[MUser.java]

```
package com.example.domain.user.model;

import java.util.Date;
import java.util.List;
import javax.persistence.JoinColumn;
import javax.persistence.ManyToOne;
import javax.persistence.Entity;
import javax.persistence.Id;

import javax.persistence.Table;
import javax.persistence.Transient;

import lombok.Data;

@Data
@Entity
@Table(name="m_user")
public class MUser {
    @Id
    private String userId;
    private String password;
    private String userName;
    private Date birthday;
    private Integer age;
    private Integer gender;
    private Integer departmentId;
    private String role;

    @ManyToOne(optional = true)
    @JoinColumn(insertable=false, updatable=false, name = "departmentId")
    private Department department;
    @Transient
    private List<Salary> salaryList;
}
```

Point1: @ManyToOne

Annotate the field with the @ManyToOne annotation to represent a many-to-one relationship. Annotate @ManyToOne because the user master table is many and the department table is one.

The optional attribute specifies whether to allow nulls for the field.

optional	null	How to join tables
true	Allow null	Left join
false	Don't allow null	Inner join

In other words, the optional attribute specifies how to join the table. The default value for the optional attribute is false.

Point2: @JoinColumn

Use the @JoinColumn annotation to specify the columns to join. This annotation is also used for table joins in one-to-one relationships.

In the name attribute, specify the column name of the join destination table.

If you use JPA's "save" method, insert / update will be executed automatically. The "insertable" and "updatable" attributes specify whether the field should be included in insert and update targets. In the sample code, it means that department is not included in insert and update.

Execution

When the user details screen is displayed, the department name will be displayed. (The execution result is omitted).

In this modification, only annotated in the field of the entity class. The method executed when displaying the user details screen remains the findById method. In other words, just by setting the relationship between entity classes, related entities will be acquired automatically.

13.3.3 Table join (one-to-many)

Overview

Next, you will learn how to join one-to-many tables.

Among the functions that must be replaced from MyBatis, the following functions remain.

Function	Correspondence
Get salary list	✓

In this section, you will create functions with a check mark for correspondence.

Directory

The directory structure is as follows. The part where the background color is changed is the new part to be added.

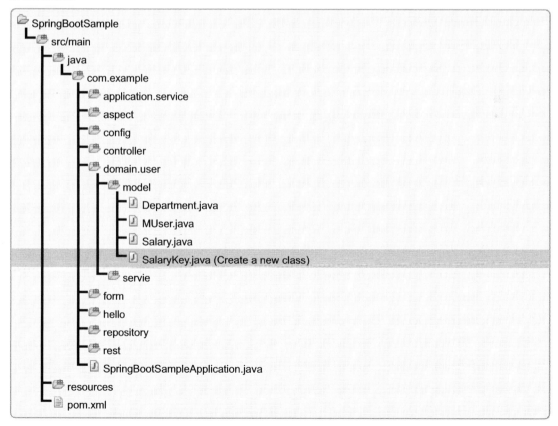

Source Code

First, create a class that represents the primary key of the salary table.

[SalaryKey.java]

```java
package com.example.domain.user.model;

import java.io.Serializable;

import javax.persistence.Embeddable;

import lombok.Data;

@Embeddable
@Data
public class SalaryKey implements Serializable {
    private String userId;
    private String yearMonth;
}
```

Point: @Embeddable

If there are two or more primary key columns, JPA needs to create a primary key class. When implementing the JpaRepository class, I had to specify the entity class and primary key class for the generics. You need to create a primary key class because you can only specify one primary key class. Annotate the primary key class with @Embeddable.

Then modify the salary entity class. The part where the background color is changed is the modified part.

[Salary.java]

```java
package com.example.domain.user.model;

import javax.persistence.EmbeddedId;
import javax.persistence.Entity;
import javax.persistence.JoinColumn;
import javax.persistence.ManyToOne;
import javax.persistence.Table;

import lombok.Data;

@Data
@Entity
@Table(name="t_salary")
public class Salary {
    // private String userId;
    // private String yearMonth;
    @EmbeddedId
```

```
    private SalaryKey salaryKey;
    private Integer salary;
}
```

Point: @EmbeddedId

The primary key field, has replaced the class you just created. When using a primary key class, annotate the field with the @EmbeddedId annotation instead of @Id.

Then modify the entity class of user master table. The part where the background color is changed is the modified part.

[MUser.java]

```
package com.example.domain.user.model;

import java.util.Date;
import java.util.List;

import javax.persistence.Entity;
import javax.persistence.Id;
import javax.persistence.JoinColumn;
import javax.persistence.ManyToOne;
import javax.persistence.OneToMany;
import javax.persistence.Table;

import lombok.Data;

@Data
@Entity
@Table(name="m_user")
public class MUser {
    @Id
    private String userId;
    private String password;
    private String userName;
    private Date birthday;
    private Integer age;
    private Integer gender;
    private Integer departmentId;
    private String role;

    @ManyToOne(optional = true)
    @JoinColumn(insertable=false, updatable=false, name = "departmentId")
    private Department department;

    @OneToMany
    @JoinColumn(insertable=false, updatable=false, name = "userId")
    private List<Salary> salaryList;
}
```

Point: @OneToMany

Annotate @OneToMany to represent a one-to-many relationship.

Since it has changed the salary entity class, and modify the user details screen. The part where the background color is changed is the modified part.

[detail.html]

```html
<!DOCTYPE html>
<html xmlns:th="http://www.thymeleaf.org"
 xmlns:layout="http://www.ultraq.net.nz/thymeleaf/layout"
 layout:decorate="~{layout/layout}">
<head>
 ...(Omitted)
</head>
<body>
 <div layout:fragment="content">
  <div class="header border-bottom">
   <h1 class="h2">User Details</h1>
  </div>
  <form id="user-detail-form" method="post" th:action="@{/user/detail}"
    class="form-signup" th:object="${userDetailForm}">
  <input type="hidden" th:field="*{userId}" />
  <!-- User Details information -->
  <table class="table table-striped table-bordered table-hover">
   ...(Omitted)
  </table>
  <!-- Button area -->
  <div class="text-center">
   ...(Omitted)
  </div>
  <!-- REST button area -->
  <div class="text-center mt-2">
   ...(Omitted)
  </div>
  <!-- Salary information -->
  <th:block th:if="*{salaryList != null and salaryList.size() > 0}">
   <div class="header border-bottom">
    <h1 class="h2">Salary</h1>
   </div>
   <table class="table table-striped table-bordered table-hover">
    <thead>
     <tr>
      <th class="w-25">Year month</th>
      <th>Salary</th>
     </tr>
    </thead>
    <tbody>
     <tr th:each="item: *{salaryList}">
      <td th:text="${item.salaryKey.yearMonth}"></td>
```

```
        <td th:text="${#numbers.formatInteger(item.salary, 3, 'COMMA')}">
        </td>
        </tr>
      </tbody>
    </table>
    </th:block>
  </form>
 </div>
</body>
</html>
```

Execution

When the user details screen of "user@co.jp" is displayed, the salary list will be displayed. (The execution result is omitted).

Note: Other relationships

In addition to many-to-one and one-to-many, the following annotations are available.

Relationship	Annotation
One-to-one	@OneToOne
Many-to-many	@ManyToMany

Summary

Here's what you've learned in this chapter.

[Overview]

- JPA automatically generates SQL, which improves development efficiency.
- Spring Data makes JPA easier to use.

[Basic]

- Creating an interface that implements JpaRepository makes it easy to create CRUD operations.
- Annotate the entity class with @Entity.
- With @Table annotations, you can change the name of the table to be mapped.
- Annotate the primary key field with @Id.
- If you prepare a method with @Query annotation, you can make an arbitrary query.
- When creating a query other than the select statement, add the @Modifying annotation as well.

[Advanced]

- If you want to change the search conditions dynamically, use the "Example" class.
- If you use ExampleMatcher, you can also execute "or condition" and "LIKE search".
- Annotate the field with the @ManyToOne annotation to represent a one-to-many relationship.
- If you want to represent a one-to-many relationship, add the @OneToMany annotation to the field.
- With @JoinColumn annotation, you can specify the column of the table join.

Appendix

As an appendix of this book, I provide the following.

- Sample source

Sample source

This section explains how to download the sample source. All the sample code created in this book is available. You can download it from the following URL.

[Download URL]
https://app.box.com/s/ryozadr164ym3zwe8qesp2mclt1fzwdd

[How to import]
How to import the sample source is as follows.

Right-click in the project explorer> select "Import"> "Import".

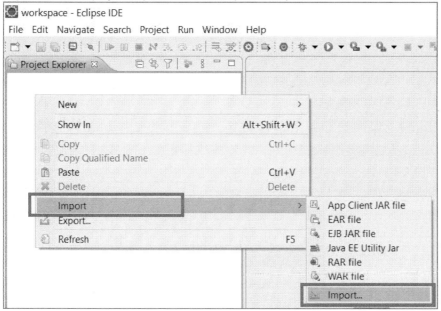

Select "Existing Maven Projects".

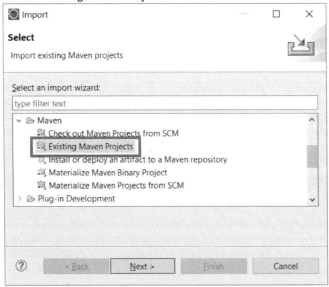

Select the downloaded folder from the "Browse" button.

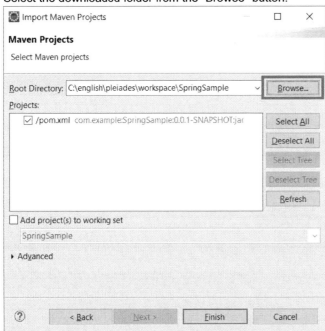

Maven will download the library, so wait a moment and the import will be complete.

In conclusion

How was this book?

Maybe you're still worried or worried about going to the actual development site. But compare you before and after reading this book. You are definitely improving your web development skills with Spring. I guarantee.

Finally there is a present. I have prepared a PDF that describes how to create the file download function. You can download it from the following URL.

[Present download URL]

https://app.box.com/s/w1l2mld5i6fyhw3sl8encx3fczks56e9
* You can download the explanation PDF and sample code from the above link.

In web development, I often use the file download function. Now you can grow further as a system engineer.

When I started learning Spring, I was in trouble because I didn't understand Spring at all. Even if I bought a book, it was boring because it was just theory, and even if I could practice it, the content was thin and I was in trouble. (And expensive). I published this book with the intention of overcoming such a situation.

I hope that you will make the most of what you have learned in this book and think that your work is fun. And if the system you develop helps others, it will make your work even more enjoyable.

Spring is a huge framework. I still have a lot to teach.

It is the most encouraging to hear your voice. Your voice encourages me to do my best in my next book. Any trivial matter is fine. Please tell us your voice.

If this book has helped you, there is no more happiness. Thank you for reading to the end.

Spring Boot Primer Second Edition

16/05/2021 First edition issued
Author Tatsuya Tamura
Contact tatsuya.tamura.business@gmail.com